GODLY BEGINNINGS
FOR
THE FAMILY

Books by Paul J. Bucknell

Allowing the Bible to speak to our lives today!

Overcoming Anxiety: Finding Peace, Discovering God

Reaching Beyond Mediocrity: Being an Overcomer

The Life Core: Discovering the Heart of Great Training

The Godly Man: When God Touches a Man's Life

The Lord Your Healer: Discover Him and Find His Healing

Redemption Through the Scriptures

Godly Beginnings for the Family

Principles and Practices of Biblical Parenting

Building a Great Marriage

Christian Premarital Counseling Manual for Counselors

Relational Discipleship: Cross Training

Running the Race: Overcoming Sexual Lusts

The Bible Teaching Commentary on Genesis: The Book of Foundations

Life Transformation: A Monthly Devotional on Romans 12:9-21

The Bible Teaching Commentary on Romans

Book of Romans: Study Questions

Book of Ephesians: Bible Studies

Abiding in Christ: Walking with Jesus

Inductive Bible Studies in Titus

1 Peter Bible Study Questions: Living in a Fallen World.

Take Your Next Step into Ministry

Training Leaders for Ministry

Satan's Four Stations: The Destroyer is Destroyed

Study Questions for Jonah: Understanding the Heart of God

Our Digital Libraries include these books as well as slides, handouts, audio/videos, and much more at: _www.foundationsforfreedom.net_

GODLY BEGINNINGS
FOR
THE FAMILY

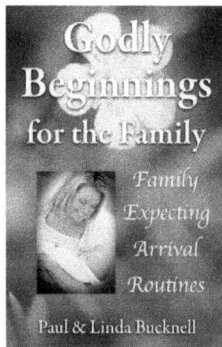

by

Paul and Linda Bucknell

Godly Beginnings for the Family: Family, Expecting, Arrival, Routines
by Paul and Linda Bucknell
Copyright © 2002,2016 by Paul J. Bucknell, Updated 2011, 2016

ISBN-10: 1-61993-043-9
ISBN-13: 978-1-61993-043-8

Digital edition
ISBN-10: 1-61993-046-3
ISBN-13: 978-1-61993-046-9

www.foundationsforfreedom.net
info@foundationsforfreedom.net

Dedication

Give glory to the mighty Father in heaven,

Who though infinite, holy and majestic,

is tender, kind and good.

May His grace, wisdom, and majestic truth

flow from our lives into our child's heart

that each child might radiate God's love on earth.

Thanks

We thank the Lord for Gary and Anne Ezzo, who served as the catalyst to get us seriously thinking about parenting, and for the many parents we have worked with since that time many years ago.

Much appreciation to Allison Bucknell, our third daughter, who did a lot to get this book ready for publishing.

Table of Contents

Preface

God loves children far more than we do. After all, they belong to Him. Even when that precious little one looks like daddy or mommy, he or she is ultimately the Creator's unique design. He has given us, the parents, a special and vital opportunity to join with Him in raising these little ones for His glory. It is our great privilege to partner with Him to care for and love these children from the day they are born, even until after they're independent. Our goal should be to prepare them to be used by God for His kingdom.

They arrive in our arms helpless and needy, ready to be shaped and molded. Whether we mean to or not, we impart our values, experiences, and hopes to our children. But beyond that, God has given us a greater purpose: to instill His love, truth, and joy in their hearts and lives.

Interestingly, the Hebrew word for children comes from the word to build. Each child is a special 'building.' In English, we call this building process "raising a child," or, more recently, parenting. Raising children might appear to look easy or natural for some, but it is not. To make parenting even more difficult, many ideas from our secular environment have influenced our own thoughts and practices, and the results have been disastrous.

In *Godly Beginnings for the Family*, we stress that good parenting always focuses on what God wants for the family. The more that parents understand God's ways and desires, the easier it will be to build children who love God and others. Even before birth, mothers consume lots of information on how to manage and love their baby. Unfortunately, much of the reading material has a strong anti-Christian bias. The information, though presented with glossy colored pictures by supposed experts, lacks instruction on what is important to God.

Even though God is the designer, many people think they can 'build' a child without His blueprint. Our burden for this book has come from our desire to pass on all that we have learned in raising eight children. We seek to enable you, the parent, by teaching you how to see God's mind and to make godly decisions before and after birth. This series brings together what God's Word says on different aspects of infant training and practical applications to various situations parents face, whether it is in a doctor's office or late at night at home when your child is crying through the night.

Our children are being built, whether we take initiative in the construction or not. God's perspective makes a great difference in how parents should look at and handle the process of birth and early infant care. We hope you will develop that perspective and train up godly children. For those with children who are beginning to crawl, walk, or throw a baseball, please read our other book, *Principles and Practices of Biblical Parenting*, written for toddlers and up; these books are designed to complement each other.

We hope not only to give them a good life on earth, but also to share His eternal life.

> Train up a child in the way he should go, even when he is old he will not depart from it (Prov 22:6).

Paul and Linda Bucknell, May 2006, Updated 2016

Godly Beginnings for the Family   FAMILY

Family Commitment

First-time parents are often full of the expectation that having a child will make their lives so much nicer and happier. And perhaps, as a bonus, they hope that having a child can solve some of their marital problems.[1] The wife might think the husband will pay more attention to the affairs of the home if they have a child, whereas the husband might hope that the wife will stop nagging him for more time because she will be busy with the child!

They should know better. Didn't they have the same kind of expectation for their marriage? Don't all married couples know that the engagement period radically differs from the actual marriage relationship? But the engaged couple believes their relationship is superior to that of other couples. The same pattern occurs with parenting.

Parents look expectantly for a joy and love that they believe a child will bring. Deep down, they believe that the child will allow a deeper bond to develop between the family and possibly bring

---

[1] There is no doubt that Jacob absorbed Isaac and Rebekah's deceitfulness and scheming. Jacob faced constant trouble as a result of his scheming, not only through Laban, but also through the bickering and manipulation of his multiple wives. Jacob's wives fought for his attention by having children. See Genesis 29:31-30:2 for a glimpse of this difficulty.

healing to their marriage's sore spots. To a degree, this works, but it's only temporary. The special joys of life, however, do not solve problems, they will only delay or modify the context in which the old problems eventually resurface. But old problems may not only be delayed by these notable life changes but may be further exasperated by them! Sleep deprivation does wonders for bringing out problems.

Heightened expectations are good and do help new parents overcome some fears that would otherwise immobilize them. When their communities pour out support and excitement, new parents are encouraged and fortified to face their new circumstances with less apprehension.

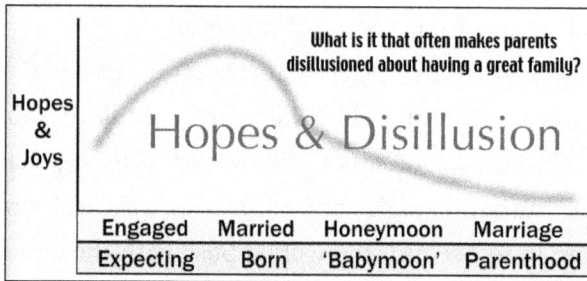

But, on the other hand, wrong expectations can lead to a lot of frustration and intense struggle. Note how the line on the above graph suddenly declines. When new parents encounter situations that are more difficult than anticipated, they can easily fall into disappointment and doubt. The dreams of a happy, excited existence are doused and reality sets in.

The key to a stable and happy family does not rest in the hope that it will all work out but in following God's plan for parenting. The displacement of hope and trust is a snag that catches many Christian parents off guard. They have hope for a fantastic family—and they should—but they do not abide by God's ways. It is dangerous to believe that good parenting just happens; the role of parents in a child's life is a deliberate design that requires the parents to follow the parenting plan that God carefully laid out.

Effective parenting depends on how closely the parents align themselves to God's design. Living by God's design requires that they first learn the instruction that God has provided in His Word. After they know God's vision for their family, they must learn to apply the scriptural principles to their family lives. Our faithfulness as parents is going to be tested, but it's essential that we follow through because the well-being of our children is at stake. Our hope in writing this book is that you can navigate safely the minefield that is parenting.

Our Goals, God's Goals

Why do people want to have children?

Children are the natural result of a man and woman's union, and regardless of societal trends that dictate how many a couple should produce, most parents have a desire for children.

Traditional answers to the question of "Why have children?" are often something along these lines: "To carry on the family name" or "It's the thing to do." Other answers might show a hidden desire where parents want their children to fulfill their personal dreams, or because of surrounding parental and societal pressures (i.e. their parents want them to have children). Of course, the ideal answer would be that they love children and want them in their lives. Why do you want children?

Most couples forget or ignore God's purpose in designing us to have children. Each woman has a large number of eggs that she is born with, which enables her to be fertile for around thirty years. Of course, God can extend this period by way of miracles (like Abraham's wife Sarah, or Elizabeth, the cousin of Mary), while He limits the childbearing ability of others.[2] But even though God might hold back children in certain situations, He is definitely pro-life. He commanded His people, "Be fruitful and multiply" in Genesis 1:22 and repeats it a few sentences later in 1:28. Even after the flood due to the great number of problems of sin in the world, God didn't change His command to "be fruitful and multiply" (Gen 8:17, 9:1,7). In other

> "As to this lower world, it was doubtless created to be a stage upon which this great and wonderful work of redemption should be transacted..."
> by Jonathan Edwards in *History of Redemption*, p. 534.

words, couples ought to focus on having many children. God's intention behind this command shows His desire for our families; He could have made things otherwise.

God commands us to procreate, but what is His purpose for the family when we do procreate? Why did He create us to desire children? When we look at the scriptures, we will discover that parents are doing a special job for God.

God's reason for commanding His people to produce a multitude of children is to cultivate a great number of people to participate in His mission to establish His kingdom on earth. These people will share in the great blessings that God wants to pour out on them throughout eternity. God simply wants to share His blessings with us and show forth His wonderful generosity.

Here are five reasons God wants godly families: (1) To exhibit a type of heaven on earth–a place where His truths are lived out in love; (2) To fully bless His people on earth and throughout eternity;

---

[2] Any couple having difficulty understanding why they cannot conceive ought to do a study of the scriptures. God says a lot regarding this. Search for womb in a concordance. Several verses speak about God closing the womb: Genesis 20;18; 1 Samuel 1:5-6.

(3) To show the amazing glory, grace, and power of His truth; (4) Extend His kingdom rule; and (5) To create a safe haven in which one can receive His protection and provision.

Note in the following verses how everyone is connected through their families to God. "For this reason, I bow my knees before the Father, from whom every family in heaven and on earth derives its name" (Eph 3:14-15).

However, this doesn't mean that every person is a child of God, though each person is made in His image. Each family gets its name from God. The phrase 'children of God' is purposely used to refer to godly people who live like their Heavenly Father. "Therefore you are to be perfect, as your heavenly Father is perfect" (Matthew 5:48).

Need for Commitment

Raising godly children in a godless world is not easy, even when you go to a great church with lots of families who are also committed to raising their families God's way. It is therefore helpful to know to what degree we are committed to raising our children in God's design. Contrary to what you may think, having children alone does not accomplish God's purpose. Many children are part of families that don't give a second thought to their impulses to satisfy materialistic or sinful desires, even Christian families. God is looking for a greater work to be done in the hearts of children through their parents' concentrated, intentional efforts.

The world's pressures, no doubt constructed by the evil one, tend to work against the godly family. Societies as a whole follow the family. This is the reason the Lord pegged the father-son relationship as the first sign of revival.

Behold, I am going to send you Elijah the prophet before the coming of the great and terrible day of the LORD. And he will restore the hearts of the fathers to their children, and the hearts of the children to their fathers, lest I come and smite the land with a curse (Mal 4:5-6).

The Lord knows that the commitment a father has to make to his sons has a direct connection to their commitment to love and serve God. This is why, when His Spirit is mightily at work, the father-child relationship is restored.

The relationships between fathers and their children are critically important. This is where children will learn respect for authority. If children do not respect their earthly fathers, then it will not be easy for them to learn to respect other authorities, including God Himself. The connection between gangs and fatherless homes is easily seen in inner cities and has been repeatedly established.[3]

But even in homes where fathers are present, close attention must be paid to the way the children are treated and trained; children with bad upbringing usually develop problems that will build up over time. This is, I believe, the largest reason for teenage rebellion. Some fathers are negligent while others authoritarian, and all ignore the needs of their children. Bitterness builds up over time and fathers exasperate this by their refusal to apologize and make amends, striping away any sense of trust between parents and children. Paul warns against this whole syndrome, "And, fathers, do not provoke your children to anger; but bring them up in the discipline and instruction of the Lord" (Eph 6:4).

Any distance between a father and child will have a huge influence on the way that same child will relate to God the Father. Even if that child becomes a Christian, he will only be able to live at a

---

[3] Just search the statistics: gangs, fatherless. There is even a website so named! https://thefatherlessgeneration.wordpress.com/statistics/

distance from God. When God works in the lives of his people (i.e. revival), they will be more capable of seeing the bitterness in their earthly relationships, and should then seek to restore them. Renewal always works itself back to the father-child relationship. This is just one of many examples that emphasizes the relationship between how you treat your children and their spiritual lives. It also helps explain why many children are leaving the Christian faith they grew up with.

When a couple has children, they are right to provide lots of love, care, and attention. Our possessions and affections have been given to us by God so that we can prepare our children for Him and His service. Your children will always have a special relationship with you, but it is critical that the vision we have for our children always rises beyond our own needs and desires, and even their needs and desires. It is great to prepare them for college, but in the end, God will not ask about what college our child attended. He is not as impressed with this as with how much time we have actually spent in good conversations with our children.

Spiritual Renewal
Malachi 4:6

FATHER ➡ CHILDREN

CHILDREN ⬅ FATHER

"He will restore the hearts of the fathers to their children, and the hearts of the children to their fathers, lest I come and smite the land with a curse."

We must prepare our children to be responsive to God. Parents are stewards of our children, given to us by God, and our job is to properly prepare our children for a life before their Designer. All of our hopes, feelings, and attention for our children must come under this understanding. We are accountable to God for how well we do the job.

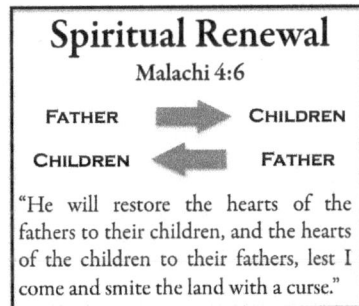

An Illustration

Let me give you an example. A mother loves dancing, and yet she could never dance the way she really wanted because she lacked proper training. She desires that her daughter would have the opportunities she didn't have, and this is fine. If she is careful to notice, however, that as a Christian mother she should detect a silent tension within her.

What should she do with this tension? On the one hand, she has a desire for her child to have great opportunities. On the other hand, she can see how the pursuit of this might lead to a conflict with the need to know, love, and serve God. Like each person, she and her daughter only have so much time. Eventually however, the conflict of priority will be revealed. What happens when that one class or competition happens to be on Sunday, the Lord's Day? Suddenly the battle will rage within their hearts. Will she take her child to church as always or will she try to convince her husband of the importance of that dance class?[4] These decisions highlight the need for us to remember that God's ways should always take a priority.

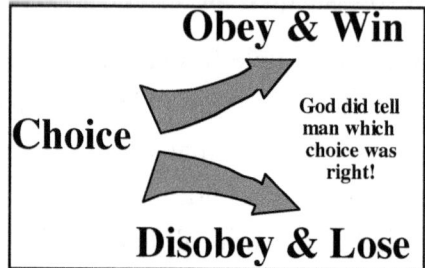

Parents are on a mission to train children to be fit members of His kingdom. God wants children who love His ways and have learned to prioritize what He wants over their own wants or desires.

---

[4] I am excited to see my children play chess. My family alone could be a small-sized chess club. But I remember the choice I made at university and later on that God's work stood as a priority. I needed to play less so that I could be faithful to my Lord's call on my own life. I need to share my story with my children and help them make the same priorities. They will see that serving God is much more important than proving my chess skills.

Opportunities to teach our children what they should value will occur over and over again. We will either teach our children to fear the Lord and love His ways or we will teach them to pursue their own goals and the pleasures of life. As parents, however, we will be held accountable to God, not the other parents in our communities. Would it not be our greatest earthly reward for a mom to have her children "rise up and bless her" (Proverbs 31:28) or to thank their dads for training them in godly ways? Parenting is lifestyle discipleship training. Food, clothes, and education are important, but we would wholly shirk our responsibility if we did not train our children spiritually. They would not be able to join God in His great program nor would they be able to share in the wonderful benefits of His eternal kingdom.

> ## *"For what does it profit a man to gain the whole world, and forfeit his soul?" (Mark 8:36)*

So what are your hopes and goals for your children? Many parents have not outwardly expressed these hopes and aspirations for their children. In many cases parents haven't even concretely thought about them. The ideas are there, and they influence the parent's decision-making process, but they often elude critical thinking.

The more we visualize our goals for our children and compare them to what God wants, the easier it will be to handle areas of potential conflict. The more clearly we understand what God wants to do through our involvement in the lives of our children, the easier it will be for us to make the needed sacrifices and ignore the

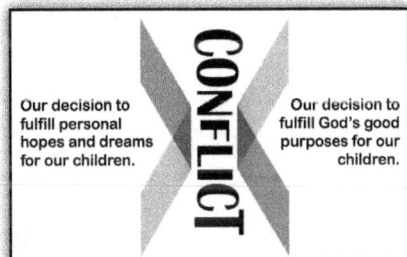

worldly pressures surrounding us. This is the way God's kingdom is established through the family. We identify His truths. We prioritize His truths. We live by His truths. We pass on His truth to the next generation.

> Let all the earth fear the LORD; Let all the inhabitants of the world stand in awe of Him. 9 For He spoke, and it was done; He commanded, and it stood fast. The LORD nullifies the counsel of the nations; He frustrates the plans of the peoples. The counsel of the LORD stands forever, The plans of His heart from generation to generation (Ps 33:8-11).

Pause for Reflection

- List at least three things you hope will happen in the lives of your children. Write down as many as you can.
- List at least three things God wants to do in your children's lives.
- Group the lists together and prioritize the list as much as is possible.

Understanding the Family from a Biblical Perspective

God has great purposes, but they have been challenged. Some cultures are more supportive of God's truths and the family than others, but no culture has avoided the war being waged on the family. Families everywhere have been captured by the god of this world. Fortunately, God reveals enough in the scriptures for us to see how the enemy works. By better understanding the attack on the family unit, we can know better how to protect our own.

From Genesis through Revelation, we will find God revealing His great purposes and plans. God prepares everything in chapters one and two: earth was created; man and woman were created;

marriage was established. God gave man a charge to establish His kingdom and rule on earth. Even the garden where man had his origins was beautifully planted in which man could live and thrive. In chapter three, however, war on earth breaks out. It had already taken place in heaven, but on earth the casualties could be counted. The family that was set up to establish God's kingdom went wayward. How was God going to carry out His plan?

The thing with God is that He incorporated provisions for the sin that would cause the first couple to go astray and for the great solution of that downfall. God had a way to establish a godly people in a world where darkness ruled. The battle would be severe and would have eternal consequences, but the more we understand this, the easier it will be to understand how the battle is fought in our own generation. First, let's look at the two sides of the war.

All Scripture portrays two sides: the godly and the ungodly.[5] All men have sinned, including the men and women who are dedicated to God's purpose. The ungodly seed has rejected God's ways. Much like godly parents pass down their faith to their children, ungodly parents will pass their religions and philosophies to their children. The first part of our civilization grew until fit for judgment. God could have destroyed this world completely, but instead He preserved a remnant to accomplish His objective. He is completing His original goals by establishing a godly seed within this dark world. It is these same individuals that God communicates with, empowers, and reveals His will to. We see this throughout the scriptures. Jonathan Edwards summarizes this by stating,

---

[5] We must refuse to be confused by thinking one country or culture is superior (or more godly/ungodly) than another. Each has its faults. It is much more important to stay fixed on how God wants us to live out our lives in our own context.

God's design was perfectly to restore all the ruins of the fall, so far as concerns the elect part of the world, by his Son; and therefore we read of the restitution of all things (Acts 3:21).[6]

God committed to this special work with a promise, and He has continued to implant these 'spoken words' throughout history to His people. The promises found in the Bible, the Word of God, bring special grace into a needy world, to create and preserve the godly ones. Genesis 3:15 contains the first promise that issues great grace to a fallen race. No person deserves this special work of God.

Genesis 3:15 "And I will put enmity between you and the woman, And between your seed and her seed; He shall bruise you on the head, and you shall bruise him on the heel."

The biblical record notes how God used key men for His purpose throughout the generations. The careful genealogical notations in Genesis and elsewhere preserve this special information, starting with the Old Testament and continuing through the New Testament (see Matthew 1) right to the end of the world as we know it. God used the family to preserve and extend the revelation of His grace, so it's no wonder that He told His people to be fruitful and multiply. The world still tugs and pulls against our families. The influence of media in all its forms makes it extremely easy for the world to connect itself to our children (while the parent doesn't even know). The impact of the smartphone on children is impossible to exaggerate as it seems to influence every aspect of a child's learning process.

---

[6] <u>History of Redemption</u> by Jonathan Edwards, p. 535.

The Collapse of a Society: A Call for Godly Instruction

Genesis 6 reveals the reason for the collapse of society and the ensuing judgment of the world. The sons of God compromised themselves and their distinct purpose of living for God. In this case, it was because the sons of God allowed their desires to rule over God's principles.[7]

> Now it came about, when men began to multiply on the face of the land, and daughters were born to them, that the sons of God saw that the daughters of men were beautiful; and they took wives for themselves, whomever they chose (Gen 6:1-2).

When God's people do not sustain their purity, God's principles and truths are corrupted and cannot be passed on in integrity. The salt has simply lost its taste and is good for nothing.[8] There is nothing left to do but toss it and start over, which is what God did through the flood. What concerns us the most is not that it happened long ago, but that Jesus said that in the last days, judgement would parallel the destruction of Noah's day.

> And just as it happened in the days of Noah, so it shall be also in the days of the Son of Man: they were eating, they were drinking, they were marrying, they were being given in marriage, until the day that Noah entered the ark, and the flood came and destroyed them all (Luke 17:26-27).

The battle has been tough from the beginning. God has accomplished a great deal through a faithful few, and God's

---

[7] For more on this compromise see www.foundationsforfreedom.net/ Topics/ WaitingOnGod/WaitUpon016.html. The evil one is using the same temptation to corrupt our own children.

[8] "You are the salt of the earth; but if the salt has become tasteless, how will it be made salty again? It is good for nothing anymore, except to be thrown out and trampled under foot by men" (Matthew 5:13).

kingdom is spread through much of the world. We need to be wise
about how the culture is seducing our children. The key is for
parents to live passionate and godly lives. Like the men of old we
must live by faith, unintimidated by the world. We need to be
committed to raising godly children, not just happy or prosperous
children.

The Preservation of God's People		
Danger	**Solution**	**Means**
Intermingled by marriage	Destroyed the wicked	Noah and the Ark
Strong power of the world	Weakened that power by isolation	Created a multilingual world
Swallowed up in pagan culture	Separated a nation from others	Called Abraham from Ur
Dependent on world power	In Egypt but separated from	Carefully placed Joseph/ Goshen

PRESERVATION OF GOD'S PEOPLE

We need to be wise. Time is short and the lives of our children are
at stake. We need to train our children to withstand the pressures
and temptations of our society. Will you commit? You need to be
decisive. Satan's temptations are too clever for us when we're
wishy-washy. When we intentionally follow the Lord, we will be
delivered from those temptations. We need brave people like
Moses' father and mother, who by faith risked their lives because
they sensed God wanted to use their son (Heb 11:23).

God will deliver our children if we sincerely seek out His ways.
Look again at the chart above on how God preserved a people for
Himself in a very dark age.

How does God pass on the truth? The most obvious way is through
our children. If our children are not impacted by the truth of God
lived out in our own lives, it's unlikely that others will be. This is

the reason the Apostle Paul made one of the qualifications for leadership the ability to manage our children and household well.

> He must be one who manages his own household well, keeping his children under control with all dignity but if a man does not know how to manage his own household, how will he take care of the church of God? (1 Tim 3:4-5).

The way we bring up our children reflects what we believe and how we live out God's truth. A man can be disqualified from ministry for not managing his household well! Some might consider this unfair, but it is not. It is common sense. If a potential leader cannot train his own children well, then he cannot successfully train others. It just won't happen. And if you try, the results will not be good.

We need to make a commitment to faithfully serve God through our families. This does not mean we ignore other ways of service, but it does mean that we need to carefully model and implement God's values and purposes at home.

Pause for Reflection

Make a prayer, with your spouse if possible, committing yourselves to raising your children according to God's design, that they might have a glorious part in God's eternal kingdom.

#1 Study Questions

1. Describe how expectations for marriage are similar to those of having a first child.

2. What does the effectiveness of parenting depend upon?

3. What are three reasons people want children?

4. What is God's purpose for us in having children?

5. What is the first sign of revival?

6. How does the relationship with one's father reflect a Christian's relationship with God?

7. How are we to resolve tensions between what we would like for our children and what God wants for their lives?

8. Is it possible that a child could gain everything we wanted for them and still fail as parents? Explain.

9. What war is described above? What does this war have to do with the family?

10. How many seeds or lines of mankind are there on earth? What are they?

11. Briefly describe the early history of the ungodly descendants.

12. Describe how God's grace is passed down through the family.

13. What does Genesis 6 say about the reason for the great collapse of the world at Noah's time?

14. What is needed in order for us to win the war against the evil one over the souls of our children?

Family Foundations

Start right, end right. This is the theme for our *Godly Beginnings for the Family.* If we do things right from the beginning, then the quality of life will be so much better. Unfortunately, and sometimes for reasons beyond our control, many of us have not started out right. In each of those cases, more time, energy, and money is necessary to straighten out the mistakes.

| Good Start | → | Good End |
| Poor Start | → | Poor End |

Once a piece of metal is bent, it cannot be perfectly restored to its original tension and shape. One example can be found in the way I set up my filing cabinet. Will I really want to improve the organization of my files after I've already stored thousands of documents? It would be best to start right. Starting a family is similar.

If we start our marriage and raise our children correctly right from the beginning, then family life works out fairly smoothly. A lack of good models and the absence of biblical teaching prevents us from seeing the necessity in making certain decisions at the beginning. Some examples are setting priorities, choosing God-pleasing paths over our self-oriented wishes, forgiving others, choosing to read the Bible over entertainment, etc. Our present parenting practices might not reflect the long-term results we wish to gain. Wisdom is the ability to make the right decisions that result in long-lasting benefits.

If we are able to discern the end result of an action or practice, then we will be equipped to make the best decisions possible. God states that wisdom stems from Him. Wisdom is readily found in His creation around us, but is especially easy to find in His Holy Word. Wisdom not only grants us a good start but also keeps us living by God's design so that the beauty of our lives can be maximized.

> *"How blessed is the man who finds wisdom, and the man who gains understanding. For its profit is better than the profit of silver, and its gain than fine gold. She is more precious than jewels; And nothing you desire compares with her." (Pr 3:13-15)*

The world is no longer family-friendly. They have lost respect for the life of the child with the legalization of abortion, and have abandoned values and truth by throwing the Bible out of the classroom. With a purpose to legitimatize their own immoral ways, the world informally and formally stands opposed to godly families. Christians are aware of this in a general way but rarely think that our own opinions, practices, or ways have been influenced by the world's secular viewpoint.

What is God's purpose for a Christian family? He wants to bring more and more people into His grand kingdom so that they can share in His eternal rewards. He calls godly parents to raise godly children so that this can become a reality. As parents, we are to instill in our children the grand vision of God's glorious holiness and love. Future chapters will show you how to practically carry this out with even the youngest babies! But first there are some issues that must be cautiously addressed as they radically shape our parenting practices and God's goals for our families.

One such issue is that of family planning. Most people—even Christians—don't even question the use of birth control. It is just assumed that newlyweds will use it. Unquestioned assumption is risky. Another issue is husband and wife roles, which is a hotly debated topic in society today.

These two issues (and there are others)[9] have only been seriously questioned in recent years. In any case, the world's thought process has penetrated our lives through our assumptions. An assumption is an idea that is believed to be true without having been proven first. It bypasses our reason and is accepted as good or normal for our lives. We would like to take this time to help you analyze your assumptions about these matters in light of God's Word. These two issues will lay a foundation for our future family life. The way we lay our family foundations will shape our marriages and greatly influence the lives of our children.

Family Planning & Birth Control

Birth control has greatly shaped our modern society. A couple now has pretty firm control over the number of children they have.[10] With abortion as a final filter, children can be selectively

---

[9] There are many areas of life that have been radically influenced by the world's system: stewardship of money and resources, the place of ease and entertainment, honor of hard work, ethics, discipleship, family devotions, missions, etc.

[10] To the dismay of many couples, of course, they discover they are not able to have children at all.

eliminated from family life.[11] Is it right to limit the number of children we have? What is the right attitude to have toward having children? Does God really care whether we have two or five children?

Most modern parents either ignore or do not think about these questions. When Linda and I were about to be married in 1978, we were fortunate to go through premarital chapters with our pastor, which was a blessing because premarital counsel was uncommon back then. One chapter had to do with birth control. The pastor never questioned its usage; he only explained how the different methods worked. In retrospect, we can see how his mindset was stained by the modern world even though he was strong on doctrine and the Word of God.

The modern mindset goes something like this: "You might want a few children, but you certainly want to control the number and spacing of them." Was there a reason the pastor declined to speak how, historically, birth control was considered immoral by Christians? Or was there a reason he failed to mention God's goal for us was to raise many godly children? Are we really supposed to control this process? Were God's people morally wrong in the past because they could not limit the number of children they had?

To be honest, we were ignorant back then. We didn't fully understand God's vision for the family and so we accepted these

---

[11] We are not saying that abortion is permissible. It is not. We must love children and repudiate any decision that would allow the Murderer to destroy or harm our children.

modern values without examining the scriptures. In fact, we didn't even know that God had an opinion on these matters or that we should look and see what God had to say more specifically about family planning. We started off poorly and this negatively affected both our attitude toward our family as well as our marriage. It has taken many years to work through this aspect of controlling and move to the point of anticipation of more children (though we feel worn out or financially unstable) and trust that God would give us what we needed in all aspects to raise godly children.

Some of you might not have ever thought about what God thinks about children. But, surprise or not, God says a lot about this issue because it is a foundational truth that shapes the way we view our lives, values, and family. What we believe will then shape what we do. The scriptures are clear about this matter. Let's examine God's purposes for giving us children in three points: God's 1) Creation mandate, 2) Covenant blessing, and 3) Loving Design.

The Creation Mandate

Most of us have heard about God's Words, *"Be fruitful and multiply"* in Genesis. Let's first read the verses and then discuss their meaning for us today. Note that the command was given to His people, the people of faith.

> And God blessed them; and God said to them, "Be fruitful and multiply, and fill the earth, and subdue it; and rule over the fish of the sea and over the birds of the sky, and over every living thing that moves on the earth (Gen 1:28).

> Bring out with you every living thing of all flesh that is with you, birds and animals and every creeping thing that creeps on the earth, that they may breed abundantly on the earth, and be fruitful and multiply on the earth (Gen 8:17).

> And God blessed Noah and his sons and said to them, "Be
> fruitful and multiply, and fill the earth" (Gen 9:1).
>
> Be fruitful and multiply; Populate the earth abundantly and
> multiply in it (Gen 9:7).

Certainly one of the things we should not do is say that God says
nothing about having small or large families. God does not say,
"You can choose to have as many children as you want." Instead
the Lord commands us to be fruitful, which can only have one
interpretation: to have large families. God tells us how we are to be
good stewards of what He has given to us. He created the first two,
but has left the rest of the population effort to us. Like any
investment, we want it to grow. The NIV translation uses the word
"increase" instead of "multiply," which covers up God's real
intention. Exodus 1:7 shows us the meaning of the word.

> But the sons of Israel **were fruitful and increased
> greatly[12], and multiplied**, and became exceedingly mighty,
> so that the land was filled with them (Ex 1:7).

This great increase of people makes a lot of sense. God wants us to
multiply abundantly, whereas the world tells us not to expand
beyond replacement levels. Replacement levels speaks only of
addition. When some die (subtraction), then we can add others to
replace them. God, however, literally tells us to multiply.[13]

---

[12] The word for increase in Exodus 1:7 actually means to swarm as in a mass number of
insects. Although not very complementary, God is very clear to its meaning.

[13] Growing economies are dependent upon a growing number of people. The world's
modern countries are showing how terrible it is to go on a 'no-growth' policy. Economies
are shrinking and elderly programs are being devastated.

However, there are a number of objections to this straightforward command. We will briefly touch on this and encourage you to read further for more extensive and up-to-date information.[14]

Argument #1: God's commands are only relevant to sparsely populated societies.

Modern man emphasizes that God's command only relates to those in sparsely populated areas. This is a reasonable argument if we strip God's purpose for giving us many children away and ignore the blessing He attaches to having lots of children. This command does not stand alone, as we will soon see. People assume that the world is over-populated (another wrong assumption), and so never seek God's perspective on this matter. God never placed a delimiter on His command to multiply. He actually wants to fill the earth with godly people. He wants mankind to spread throughout the earth, even into the suburbs and countryside. God wants to see the resources that He provided used well!

Secular man has taken it upon himself to fix the problem. We are aghast at some of the steps societies have taken to control the population of the world, including the sterilization of large groups of people.[15] Our own country subsidizes sterilization in poorer

---

[14] There are many books being written on the myths of the 'over-population' theories. The clearest is that we are still living! (Some have predicted that we would have already run out of food.) The War Against Population by Jacqueline Kasun (Ignatius Press) is one excellent resource to get the facts. Mary Pride in her The Way Home traces her path of how she, once a formerly feminist woman, has now come to live by God's Word (Crossway Books).

[15] "1976: Government admits forced sterilization of Indian Women". https://www.nlm.nih.gov/nativevoices/timeline/543.html

countries.[16] Man wars against God's purposes. They are willing to kill children, but are proud to preserve the spotted owl and other endangered species.

Argument #2: There are not enough resources on earth to provide for a multiplying population.

Man has a fear that the earth's resources are insufficient or limited. Our real problem has not been insufficient resources. Even today, huge USA government programs pay farmers **not** to produce food.[17] War, greed, and some religious sects are our true problems. God uses famine and pestilence to direct people back to Himself. Famines are mostly due to war and greedy leaders. God says that these natural disasters are a result of disobedience.

As man multiplies, he will be able to specialize his studies and become much more resourceful. This, in turn, enables him to make more progress in developing God-given resources. My friend recently asked me what it takes to grow crops, and the answer is simple: plants need the sun and water and a few minerals to grow and produce. Yet in this day and age, it's even possible to grow luscious tomatoes in a green house without soil at all.[18]

As to land, we still have plenty of land to live on. Back in the 80s when my family and I lived in Taiwan, it was one of the most densely populated areas on earth. Many people moved down from the mountains to the cities. We lived many floors higher than we were used to, but life was very doable. When people are polite and abide by good social laws, everyone can live peacefully together.

---

[16] "United States is Funding Sterilization Camps Targeting Women in India". http://www.lifenews.com/2015/01/13/united-states-is-funding-sterilization-camps-targeting-women-in-india/

[17] "Downsizing the Federal Government." http://www.downsizinggovernment.org/agriculture/subsidies

[18] "Hydroponics." https://afsic.nal.usda.gov/aquaculture-and-soilless-farming/hydroponics

God never wanted us to live in fear but in trust in Him. Many so-called environmentalists do not trust God because they are scared. They should learn from Malthus; back in the 1700s, he first logged his theory about how perilous man's situation was because the population was increasing faster than sparse resources! God, however, embarrasses man's theories by abundantly providing for the needs of the earth.[19] People's creative solutions are everywhere, including the economically viable means of converting seawater to fresh water.

Argument #3: The world is too evil to bring up children.

The world is evil; it always has been, and always will be. But even here we need to remember God's promises. What about Daniel, who was raised in captivity? And what about Moses, who was just barely saved from baby slaughter by parents who risked their lives? We forget it is God who blessed Israel while they were in captivity in Egypt! Because of God's public policy to greatly increase the Israelites' population, the Egyptians came up with their own form of birth control–murder (Exodus 1). God has worked in difficult circumstances before such as we find in Exodus. How else could three million people survive as they slowly traveled through barren land? The Lord can do what is needed in our era of billions of people too.

This is an area in which we need to check our attitudes. How we start with our children will affect them for the rest of their lives. For example, what parent hasn't thought of the safety of his or her child? We all do. But our response is critical. Either we will instill an outlook of faith or of fear into our child's life. Dangers will be present; sometimes worse than at other times or places. Having a

---

[19] "... Thomas Malthus' Essay on the Principle of Population (1798) ... must be one of the curiosities of our age that though Malthus' forecast has proved mistaken that, in fact, the living standards of the average person have reached a level probably unsurpassed in history–doom is still pervasively forecast." –Kasun, p.26.

faith in God who will care for them is invaluable in such circumstances. Our child will gain this same faith as we trust God to care for them.

If we are married, then we need faith not only for our lives but also for our children. In most cases the fear is worse than the actual threat. Nevertheless, we must live or die in faith; there is no other option. We can't stop having children because of a decadent society with bursts of terrorism or threats of war.[20]

Are children a burden?

From the phrase "Be fruitful and multiply," we can understand a few things about God. He is pro-life in every sense of the word. He designed and provided for life. God is like a salesman who encourages each of us to take part in this wonderful, life-building program. God commanded it to generate the fruition of His plan. We have no option but to be positive about having children, even lots of them.

We have noticed that a certain negative or 'burdensome' attitude is quite common among modern parents. They are so busy with their lives and careers that caring for their children has become a hassle. They don't enjoy them. This mentality sometimes originates with our own parents, when *we* were unwanted children. You might remember your mother groaning about doing so much work for you and telling you how unappreciative you were for it. We might even remember words like 'You were a big mistake' or 'Did I ever tell you that we never planned on having you?' Words like these can leave big scars. These kinds of statements have wounded many children. Others are so busy creating lives of ease, wealth, or fame

---

[20] Paul in 1 Corinthians 7:26 states that the way to hold back from having children in difficult situations is simply not to get married. "I think then that this is good in view of the present distress, that it is good for a man to remain as he is."

that they don't want to serve others, much less their own children. This is pure selfishness.

The solution for our supposed problems is found right here in these verses. By meditating on "Be fruitful and multiply," we will gain God's grand perspective of life. We need to see that each life is valuable and that God wants us around. Death was necessary because of sin, but God is so pro-life that He made a way for us to come back to life again! If you feel like you were an unwanted child, or feel your children are burdensome to you, deal with it or your perspective will negatively impact your children. Sometimes we need to forgive our parents. At other times we need to repent for trying to carry out our own plans independently from God's purpose for our lives. If we do not start right, there will be many undesirable consequences.

Summary

God desires us to intentionally further His cause with our wills and bodies. He has given most of us, like Adam and Noah, the ability to have multiple children. God put no limit on His command, He has never rescinded it, and we see that He wants us to have more children rather than less. Should we really take the opportunity to limit the number of children we produce? No. We should be open to having as many children as He would want to give us. He wants to fill this earth with people who seek Him.

God miraculously provides for those who trust Him.

A pair of pants for an active boy.

Money for a car to replace our dead one.

Gas money to visit grandparents.

Special treats to remind us that He is watching out for us.

Timely financial assistance.

This creation mandate is given to all of us to steer our mindset, which should influence our particular decisions. Yes, it is God's will for some to stay single. Yes, some couples can't have children, but still the mandate pushes us forward into God's purposes. God's intent is that we all get serious about having lots of children and raising them for His glorious purposes. Let's look at how God has associated blessing with lots of children.

Covenant Blessing

One of the most humorous situations in life can be found in how modern man looks for profit, success, and blessing in every part of his life, save that of children. Man is so caught up in materialism and comfort that he doesn't even like to think about having many children; some end up choosing not to have any children.

Other parents are being tricked to think only of the hurdles that come with raising children. They hear the stories about how it takes two adult parents to feed or diaper one little child. This might sound ridiculous, but to be honest, parents who do not parent God's way find that their modern techniques and assumptions create intolerable living situations.[21] A better solution is to learn how to raise children God's way. God's view is radically different: children are a blessing, not a burden! Let's look at a few scripture verses that show God's attitude toward children.

---

[21] Advanced education is a luxury not a necessity. When we make it a necessity of life, then in some societies and situations, the financial burden causes undue pressure on the family even having some parents make a tragic decision to live apart from each other so both can work. God is much more interested in creating godly values in our children than educated one's loaded with debt.

> Your wife shall be like a fruitful vine, within your house, Your children like olive plants around your table. Behold, for thus shall the man be blessed who fears the LORD (Ps 128:3-4).

> Let our sons in their youth be as grown-up plants, and our daughters as corner pillars fashioned as for a palace (Ps 144:12).

> Behold, children are a gift of the LORD; The fruit of the womb is a reward. Like arrows in the hand of a warrior, So are the children of one's youth. How blessed is the man whose quiver is full of them; They shall not be ashamed, When they speak with their enemies in the gate (Ps 127:5).

God's blessing is associated with having lots of children. This is the natural and proper way to think of families. In our day and culture in the United States, it might be odd to speak of larger families, but it was only one or two generations ago that most people had large families. When there is harmony in the home, children from large families have the most fun. They always have several playmates. Low incomes don't matter as much as we make it out to be. I still fondly remember the games I used to play with my brother and sisters.

The reluctance of some parents to have many children stems from the supposedly exorbitant cost of raising even one child. They cannot understand how raising a child to the age of seventeen, at a cost of over US$240,000, can possibly be a blessing.[22] They think of it as next to impossible. The odd thing is, the richer people are, the fewer children they have! How can something with such a high price tag be a blessing? I suppose the answer should be a question, "Who are you going to trust?"

---

[22] Adjusted for inflation reaches over $300,000. http://www.usda.gov/wps/portal/usda/usdahome?contentid=2014/08/0179.xml&contentidonly=true Interestingly they add, "Expenses per child decrease as a family has more children."

We must choose to listen to God's Word. God says blessings are associated with being godly and having children. When we put the pieces together, we can see that God wants godly families to have lots of children. Can you read it any other way?

For clarification, let's look at how God frames His covenant with His people. Deuteronomy 28 lists the blessings and the curses of the covenant. Blessings come from obeying His laws; curses come from disobeying His laws. Blessings are typically shown through productivity, including the bearing of children.[23] God does not separate the blessing of wealth from the blessing of children. They go together. In other words, if there are many children, there will also be enough resources to support and grow them.[24]

Obedience & Blessing	Disobedience & Curse
"The LORD will establish you as a holy people to Himself, as He swore to you, if you will keep the commandments of the LORD your God, and walk in His ways" (Deuteronomy 28:9). "And the LORD will make you abound in prosperity, in the offspring of your body and in the offspring of your beast and in the produce of your ground..." (Deuteronomy 28:11).	"But it shall come about, if you will not obey the LORD your God, to observe to do all His commandments and His statutes with which I charge you today, that all these curses shall come upon you and overtake you" (Deuteronomy 28:15). "Cursed shall be the offspring of your body and the produce of your ground, the increase of your herd and the young of your flock" (Deuteronomy 28:18).

BLESSING AND CURSE

---

[23] At times God closes the womb for reasons other than disobedience. In the case of Jacob's wife Rachel, it was chastisement. In Hannah's case (Samuel) it was to cause them to dedicate their child to the Lord. When we think of God's blessing upon a marriage, we should think about multiple godly children.

[24] Part of the problem is the expectation of some that parents need to provide a college education for all of their children. My perspective is that God will provide what they are need–not all need college. I have found this true with 8 children, though some still have not reached college age.

The world's way to plan a family is to guess at how many children a couple can be handled emotionally and financially, balancing their decision on how many they think they can handle. God hates the selfishness, self-confidence, and lack of faith by which parents make these decisions because they are not open to be used as God desires. Children suffer emotional and physical problems from not feeling wanted. How much we need God's perspective!

God wants us to be eager to have children! He wants us to not only desire to have one or two children to satisfy our inner needs, but to raise lots of godly children. We are to trust God for grace, wisdom, love, and wealth to raise 'His' children. If God doesn't want us to have more children, then surely He knows how to close the womb.

Those who use various birth control methods often doubt the depth of God's involvement in the lives of the children they receive from Him. Instead of seeing themselves as the source of life, they need to see God as the Giver of life and the Provider who cares for those children. Our generation should shirk its fears and join former generations who demonstrated the faith it took to raise large families in much more challenging days and to look forward to the ways God will raise up many godly children through their committed lives, bringing glory to His Name. The world will heartily reject the reasoning behind the rearing of large families, but it is a definite blessing of a godly marriage to have many children.

Personal Testimony

My wife and I did not begin our family with a vision for what God wanted for us, but He worked with us and slowly opened our eyes. We thought we were smart missionaries by only having two children. What a sham! Upon our return home, God began to teach us the basics of what God wanted a family to look like from His Word, as well a number of other books.[25]

Our family's 'second generation' (six children between 1991-2001) happened by the grace of God. Instead of considering children a disruption to God's purpose in our lives, we learned to believe that they were a necessary means for God to reveal His gospel to the world. We committed to training them to be arrows that God could use to bring glory to His Name.

There were many things that happened to make us uneasy about the call to a large family: several miscarriages, no guaranteed monthly salary, and no savings. There were many days when we didn't know where the next day's milk would come from. By no means am I suggesting that others should live like us, but it is comforting to have lived a life of faith where God's provision was intimately evident.

God used our humble circumstances to show that money should never be a reason for having fewer children—even when living in a large modern city with the demands of a modern world. God has provided for us step by step, which included sending several children through college, and helping a few others with their expenses as they transition into their lives as independent adults. He has shown Himself marvelous in the way He has provided for us.

---

[25] Here are two good books: A Full Quiver by Rick & Jan Hess: Family Planning and the Lordship of Christ, 236 pp. Wolgemuth & Hyatt, Publishers, 1989; 1749 Mallory Lane, Suite 110, Brentwood, Tennessee 37027.
Children: Blessing or Burden: Exploding the Myth of the Small Family by Max Heine, Creation House, 1989, 224 pp

On another positive note, deciding not to use birth control measures[26] has saved us a lot of money, inconvenience, and distraction. We could finally focus on fully expressing our love to each other in faith rather than in fear. We had our concerns: we were older, with less youthful vigor, financial uncertainty, and a busy life. As soon as we decided to trust God with our reproductive life, though, these were no longer worries because we trusted that our God knew what we could handle. In that step of faith, we sensed that love blossomed in both our lives as well as in our children's lives. Meanwhile, our faith was set on Him, as it ought to be, to help us raise eight godly children who are devoted to Him and His ways.

Loving Design

What is God really up to? What is His final goal? Let's look at the end of the Bible.

> After these things I looked, and behold, a great multitude, which no one could count, from every nation and all tribes and peoples and tongues, standing before the throne and before the Lamb, clothed in white robes, and palm branches were in their hands (Rev 7:9).

God is raising up a great people who will form the Bride of Christ. They will continue reigning where Adam stopped. In a sense, it is happening right now through God's people on earth. But in the new heavens and earth, the Bride will be united. God desires a great multitude to join Him in sharing His rich eternal blessings.

---

[26] If you use birth control, you should be aware not only of the moral dangers but also the physical dangers. Moral dangers include greater temptation to promiscuity and the cultivation of fear in the life and relationship of a couple. Some birth control devices can physically harm our bodies (some find that it is hard to re-regulate their bodies after using certain types of birth control so that they can have children).

God expands His kingdom program through the multiplication of His people. It is obvious that God intends His people to properly raise their children. Fathers are told to "bring them up in the discipline and instruction of the Lord" (Eph 6:4). Mothers are to "bear children" (1 Tim 5:14).[27] As a natural result of faithful parenting and instruction in the Lord, a lot of children will come to love Him. This is nothing new. The Old Testament speaks of this in several places, though particularly in Deuteronomy 6. It is tragic when it doesn't happen.

If we refuse to raise godly children, how will God's kingdom expand? Yes, of course there is the missionary endeavor, which is right and good. But does it make any sense to focus on missionary expansion out there and ignore raising our own godly children? The best way is to do both. God has enabled most parents to have children, and they have a responsibility to bring them not only into the world but into God's family. Should we not more willingly and devotedly raise and disciple our own children?

I remember once playing with my two year-old. The thought came to me, "What would have happened if I never had this child?" It would have been a tragedy borne out of caution, fear, or self-indulgence had I chosen not to have this child. It is easier to think about not having children when there is no associated face. I hate to think of how my sin might have caused us to have one or two fewer children.

Summary

Let us no longer think that having or not having children is inconsequential to God and His plan. Satan is known as the murderer and deceiver. He is just as glad not to have the children

---

[27] Although Paul addresses the widow here, it is obvious that bearing children is right and proper in the Lord's sight.

born to Christian parents as to have the chance to later eliminate them. As Christian parents, we are privileged to expand God's kingdom by working hard and diligently in raising our children in the Lord.

Father and Mother Roles

One of the biggest reasons for conflict and bitterness in the family today is a result of the conflict of husband and wife roles. Conflict, tension, and arguments occur because of expectations that rise from assumptions we carry without knowing it. Again, this was not as much a problem in the past when roles were more clearly defined than they are today. But nothing seems straightforward today except that everyone should do their own thing!

God has given us great instructions in His Word regarding the function of husbands and wives.

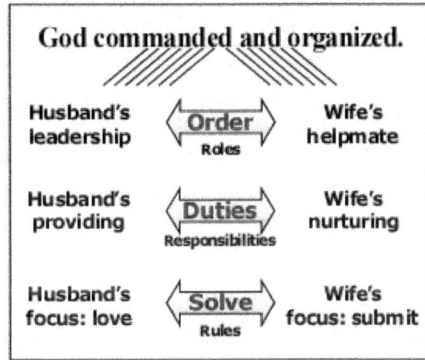

Christians, however, often miss God's instructions in this area of life because they are comfortable with their set of worldly assumptions. God is very concerned with how our children are raised. How we raise them is greatly impacted by how we carry out our roles in the home. How we start will impact the final result. We cannot give a full treatment of this subject here, but let us focus on helping you biblically understand three kinds of couples.

Scenario #1: Odd Couple

This husband and wife are confused. They are convinced that, for each other's benefit, they should take turns being husband and wife. The wife wants to be fulfilled and have a career. She wants to have her freedom to roam and spend time and energy outside the home.

Meanwhile, the man thinks that in order to be a loving husband he is to be a mother for a while and give his wife a break. The hidden assumption here is that motherhood is less of a calling than a career outside the home. Although the husband couldn't be pregnant, he did wear a sack to help him sympathize with his wife. He has taken leave from work to care for the baby. Of course, he can't nurse the baby either, but he can feed him/her with a bottle. There is a silent war between them. They can pretend that they are both happy, but both are guilty and distressed.

What is God's advice? The wife is to come home to mother as the scripture mandates. The husband is to believe that God has designed the mother to be enriched through her important mothering role.

> Older women likewise are to be reverent in their behavior, not malicious gossips, nor enslaved to much wine, teaching what is good, that they may encourage the young women to love their husbands, to love their children, to be sensible, pure, workers at home, kind, being subject to their own husbands, that the word of God may not be dishonored (Tit 2:3-5).

Mothers are clearly to be workers at home. They need to be busy doing the things that God has specially created them to do.

- Women are designed to have children (Gen 3:16; 4:1-2).
- Women alone are designed to nurse a baby with the right kind of nutritious fluids (1 Thes 2:7; Song 8:1).

- Women are designed to be relationship-focused so that they can find fulfillment from caring for children (1 Thes 2:8).
- Women are designed to be tender, soft, smooth, and round with a sweet voice to comfort and care for an infant (Song 2:14).

Men on the other hand should find a job that provides for his household. He is not to be lazy but diligent so that his family does not suffer.

- Men are designed to work in order to provide for their household and help contribute to the welfare of society (1 Tim 5:8; 1 Thes 2:9-11; Gen 3:17-19).[28]
- Men are made to be strong so they can fight, work hard, and protect their families and countries from the enemy (1 Tim 6:12; Num 1:22; Song 3:8).
- Men are designed to be leaders who are able to pass instruction on to others (1 Tim 2:12-13; 1 Thes 2:10-11; Deut 6:1-7).

Scenario #2: Semi-Modern Couple

The semi-modern husband and wife make a real effort to have a good, healthy marriage. From the outside, everything seems well, but several troublesome spots lay submerged, gnawing at them. These conflicts come from not clearly working out the roles of the husband and wife.

As long as responsibilities are not clearly defined, spouses can become aggravated with each other. The wife might expect the husband to help care for the child, whereas the husband keeps hinting at how the wife can get a job to help relieve the financial situation. Deep down, they become bitter because the other spouse

---

[28] The Chinese character for male has two parts: a field and a symbol for strength or power.

is not fulfilling the other's expectations. Their relationship works, but it is tense and unhappy.

What is God's advice? The couple needs to recognize and straighten out several issues regarding their marriage.

(1) Responsibilities flow from your role.

The husband and wife should be able to clearly mark their areas of responsibility. They should not expect the other spouse to help except for emergencies. For example, the husband should get a good sleep to perform well at work (he should not have to wake up in the middle of the night to bring the two-week-old baby to Mom to nurse). The wife should care for the children's needs. The husband, of course, should help out especially when he sees a need. This is love in action. The wife should not begrudge her husband if he doesn't help her, but instead look to God for strength, wisdom, and love to help the crying child.

The husband should take all pressure off the wife to work outside the home. He should instead support her in her efforts in the home. He needs to provide instruction for the home and children and should not expect his wife to do this. He needs to care for the needs of the house. In either case, neither of them should demand or expect the other to fulfill responsibilities that are their own.

My wife and I understand our roles as such: the husband cares for financial provision from outside the home and cares for the house itself, while the wife's roles derive from care for her husband and the children that includes cooking, cleaning, and care. Each spouse has his/her natural talents that can be put to use—whether it be a husband cooking or a wife doing the accounts—but a couple needs to carefully define their expectations and be faithful in doing them. Proverbs 31 helps us see how an industrious wife—without neglect to her family—bought and sold property, but the wife should never put her responsibility to her husband and children aside for career sake.

(2) Solve issues

When a spouse senses tension because of what the other spouse is or is not doing, he or she should go before the Lord to discern where the expectations or frustrations are coming from before they confront the spouse. For instance, if a wife finds herself distant from her husband, she should understand that there might be a problem hiding deeper in her heart than she expects. The same is true when a man gets angry.

Get beneath the surface and figure out why you might be getting easily angered. We understand that not all problems are because of different expectations of responsibility, but many are.

Once the problem is figured out, you should see if you should adjust your expectations. If your love doesn't seem to 'cover a multitude of sins', then you need to talk about the problem at a convenient and private time. The husband needs to speak gently so that the wife can understand the issue. He should give her time to think and sort out her feelings. The wife needs to respectfully bring the issue to her husband's attention and allow him to lead the discussion.[29]

For example, tension could occur over the husband's dislike for the way the wife conducts her housecleaning. He thinks the house is cluttered or dirty. He should first express appreciation for her work but kindly suggest how she might do a better job with cleaning. He might need to kindly and patiently pinpoint what he doesn't like and the reason why. She might not have thought of it as a problem.

---

[29] The husband might refuse to discuss the issue. This is the husband's prerogative. It does not mean it is best, but it does mean the wife should not nag but trust God for wisdom, joy, and grace in such situations.

When he sees her faithfulness to him, he should take notice and encourage her.

There was a time my wife mentioned the slow laundry sink drain. I sensed some tension in my heart when she mentioned it. As I thought about it, my frustrations were partly about how the problem recurs, and I tried not to let that irritant affect my response to her. There's a temporary solution: pour some acid down the drain. I thought, "She can do that!" To me, this situation could be classified as part of the housework. But then, as I continued to think through the matter, I remembered the acid's strength and her hesitancy to handle it. Instead, I chose to cheerfully deal with it.

(3) Anticipating change in new situations

A couple facing something new should realize that tension might increase because responsibilities are changing, or their physical and emotional stamina are challenged. Ideally, whoever points out the need, the husband should lead a discussion on how this might affect the family. This might be a simple situation like the whole family beginning to regularly attend a Friday night meeting, or special times like having a baby. If it is something like the latter, the husband should make sure his wife has some extra help, whether it means having a grandma come by or that he just pitches in more.

The husband and wife's distinct roles do not imply that a duty is below the dignity of the other. The husband can change a diaper. The wife can take out the garbage. The point of roles is to help each spouse know and faithfully fulfill his or her responsibility. Our roles remind us also that the husband and wife should be content with what God has given them to do on earth. The wife must be at peace being home and forget about the world's inference that she is not doing her best or that she is missing out on life. This does not mean she cannot contribute to some neighborhood meeting, church ministry, or pursuit her extra-household interests, but marriage and her role as a mother should come first. Master them with God's strength, and you can extend yourself as God leads. Some great passions might need to wait for another season of your life. It is part of the way we die to ourselves and find greater meaning in our dedication. Our roles are designed by God according to gender and roles in our marriages and society as stated in the above scriptures.

Scenario #3: Biblical Model

In a healthy marriage relationship, a husband and wife will love to be married; they will love to be together. So what comprises a good marriage? This is not a book on marriage, but the existence and quality of the marriage are the greatest shapers of the family. Marriage is defined as a couple committed to each other, enabling them together to properly take up their God-appointed roles without shirking their responsibilities and, when differences occur, they will know how to resolve the trouble. Kind communication is important for both sharing vision, frustration, finding support, and resolving differences of opinion.

Ephesians 5 provides reminders to both husband and wife because our selfish sin nature continually pulls couples away from God's purposes. The husband finds many avenues for expressing His love including genuine acknowledgement and care for his wife. A wife will be glad of the leadership that her husband has over the home, especially when it comes to teaching their children about the Lord. He ought to be up before work, meeting with the Lord and praying for his family and other matters. The husband makes sure he pays attention to special needs around the home.

The wife remembers her calling to be her husband's helpmate. She is, of course, largely outfitted to bring children into the world and nurture them. One of the greatest foes of marriages and good parenting is a feminism that rejects God's purposes for the wife and mother. God reminds the wife to be subject to her husband to protect her and the family. Many women have left, physically or emotionally, the devotion to be a wife and mother, believing she will be fulfilled by being like a man. As long as this disbelief over God's 'family planning' continues, wives will find themselves discontent and seek things beyond the home to satisfy. Proverbs 31 again points us to contentment in the home and service outside as one gives opportunity.

What is God's advice?

Keep it up! God delights in good marriages. There are two keys to a good marriage: (1) Faithfulness in carrying out your responsibilities, and (2) rightly and lovingly relating and responding to your spouse.

Clearly defined and kept roles help clarify responsibilities and minimize conflict. Close attention to our duties becomes the way we faithfully live before God, bringing the hope of bearing good fruit in our marriages and children.

Having a clear understanding of and the ability to apply God's commands for the husband and wife will enable a couple to communicate well when there are misunderstandings. They have a way to discuss problems and leave them in God's hands. When the husband leads well, it is easy for the wife to follow. The husband needs to focus on loving his wife. This means that he ought to seek out practical and deliberate ways to show his love to her. He must consider her needs and meet them, which can include something as basic as praying for her.

The wife is designed to be her husband's helpmate. When she has a greater understanding of how she fits into the role God created her for, it becomes easier for her to submit and work hard at doing what would please her husband and God. A wife's reluctance to submit to her husband produces ongoing tension and friction.

Summary

When a couple faithfully follow scriptural guidelines for marriage, they provide a beautiful model for their child to learn from, in addition to reaping great benefits in their marriage and family. If couples do not start out right, misunderstandings will quickly develop between them. Bitterness will be stored up and a wall of mistrust built. This distance will eventually lead to all sorts of hardships in the marriage, which will be transferred to the children. By starting off right, however, our children will instead learn love, respect for authority, self-control, and conflict resolution.

#2 Study Questions

1. Fill in the blanks. _____ right, _____ end.

2. What is wisdom?

3. Why is assumption so dangerous?

4. What is the modernist family-planning attitude?

5. Memorize one of the verses above that mention, "Be fruitful and multiply."

6. What kinds of fear come up when people hear of over-population? What is one example of what people have done in response to this fear?

7. Are there really enough resources for a multiplying population? How can we be sure?

8. How does Exodus 1 show us how difficult situations should not hold couples back from having children?

9. How do we generally expect to see God express His blessing to His faithful people?

10. Why does God want Christians to have a lot of children?

11. What can cause a large amount of marital conflict?

12. Why do couples have such different perspectives of how they should carry out their duties?

13. What is the solution?

14. What are at least two special ways in which God has designed the woman? How do they reflect themselves in the roles God asks her to carry out at home?

15. What are at least two special ways God has designed the man? How do they reflect themselves in the roles God asks him to carry out?

16. What are the two keys for a good marriage?

17. What special commands does God give for the husband and wife to follow to keep a good relationship?

18. How does the way a husband and wife relate to each other affect their children?

Godly Beginnings for the Family EXPECTING

God's Family Health Plan

Most people never think of the Bible as a health book. But, surprise! It is. There are so many teachings and examples that will stun the modern reader when they begin to seriously think about the implications. We sterilize God's teaching with spiritual jargon, treating it as though it has nothing to do with our daily lives, but God has tied health to obedience. Lack of good health can sometimes be a sign of disobedience, discipline, or judgment.[30]

God has provided many guidelines in His Word so that we can have and maintain good health. God has designed our bodies to live long and healthy lives; God wants us to be healthy people! Parents are responsible before God to properly care for their own bodies to set an example for their children in good stewardship and to care for their children's health.

---

[30] Some people would say all sickness is from sin, but there are cases such as the Apostle Paul's problem and Timothy's stomach problems that do not allow such conclusions.

A puzzle?

Have we ever thought about where plants come from? Who was it that gave expert advice on dietary laws? Where do we learn how to successfully deal with relational problems? How are we able to conquer our fear and anxieties? Where do we learn about bodily healing and the inner cleansing of our souls? Our Designer provided the key to good health through His Word and world. For example, many of the plants that we identify as weeds are actually herbs. God has built in much more healing into this world than we understand.[31] We are not promised perfectly healthy bodies, but when we take His Word seriously, many problems that we would otherwise encounter are no longer an issue.

About 150 years ago in a famous Vienna hospital, one out of every six new mothers died. In the obstetrical ward, Ignaz Semmelweis made an astounding observation that changed healthcare forever: he noted a connection between which mothers died and the teachers and students who examined them. Based on his observations, he suggested that the students who touched corpses should wash their hands before they did anything else. After this rule was implemented, only one out of every forty-two women died in the first month alone. He then recommended that they all go a step further: all doctors, students, and nurses should wash their hands between living patients. He was ridiculed for this and lost his job as a result.[32]

Today, we know the importance of hand washing, as inconvenient as it may be at times. Many deaths could have been avoided if the

---

[31] "In the middle of its street. And on either side of the river was the tree of life, bearing twelve kinds of fruit, yielding its fruit every month; and the leaves of the tree were for the healing of the nations" (Rev 22:2).

[32] None of these Diseases by S.I. McMillen (Revell Press, 1963), pp. 15-17.

medical community had simply followed the principle of God's careful instructions given back 2000 B.C.:

> The one who touches the corpse of any person shall be unclean for seven days (Num 19:11).

> Now when the man with the discharge becomes cleansed from his discharge, then he shall count off for himself seven days for his cleansing; he shall then wash his clothes and bathe his body in running water and shall become clean (Lev 15:13).[33]

God gave them proper hygienic techniques including washing under running water rather than in a still basin, washing and changing clothes, and time intervals to allow the sun to kill bacteria that was not washed off. As God's children, we have inherited this precious volume, which includes many special insights for living healthy lives.

God wants us to have godly and healthy children. We understand that we live in a sin-cursed world and that some run off from it will impact both our lives and the lives of our children, but we should make an effort to minimize this impact and increase God's touch on our lives by seriously considering biblical instruction and caution.

Having your first child is the beginning of a new adventure. New parents are open to rethinking their lifestyles and choices. Let's take a look at God's family health plan for His people. Here are two questions to keep in mind as your read: 1) What are its benefits? 2) What are its costs?

---

[33] Please note we are not saying it is by observing these commands that we gain acceptance from God. We live under the new covenant through Jesus Christ. This does not mean, however, that we should neglect wisdom gathered from these laws.

The Benefits of God's Health Plan

I will put none of the diseases on you which I have put on the
Egyptians; for I, the LORD, am your healer (Ex 15:26).

The ancient Egyptians had health books just like we do, though of
course in different form![34] They listed the symptoms, diseases, and
possible cures of those diseases. God desired the Israelites to be free
from all of the diseases that the Egyptians were afflicted with. God
desired for His people to live above the many problems that were in
the world. By pointing out the Egyptians' problems, He meant for
His people to turn to Him as the Healer. They needed only to
know God's commands and obey! The same is true of the world
today; many diseases originate in sinful habits and anxieties. The
promise sounds good, but what is the catch? Does it just apply to
the Israelites? What did they have to do?

The Cost of God's Family Health Plan

And He said, "If you will give earnest heed to the voice of the
LORD your God, and do what is right in His sight, and give
ear to His commandments, and keep all His statutes (Ex 15:26).

The price of God's health plan is rather obvious, or at the very
least, plain and straightforward. There was no small print. He
wanted obedience. If His people obeyed His laws, He would care
for them both directly and also through the laws He built into
creation. On the other hand, if they were not faithful, their
coverage would be discontinued. In the same way, God will not
cover for our sinful behavior. God said it was for our good and for
our survival that we follow His commands. I am not saying a
person needs to follow the Old Testament dietary laws, but we do

---

[34] There are two ancient Egyptian papyrus rolls that informs us of these things: The Eber
Papyrus (110 pages long) and the Edwin Smith Papyrus (17 pages long).

need to recognize that there is much to learn from our loving and wise God in the Word that He's provided for us.

> "To observe all these statutes, to fear the LORD our God..." → "for our good always and for our survival."
>
> ## Obedience brings blessings!
> **Deuteronomy 6:24-25**

But to which commands and statues is He referring? What do they have to do with our well-being? If we aren't Jewish, does this apply to us? Before anything else, I want to be extremely clear: we are not discussing salvation. Salvation is by faith in Christ Jesus, not in our works. We can't "go to heaven" by living according to the law because we are sinners and are inherently unable to follow the law. We are, however, meant to live out our salvation.[35] These commands are meant to help us get a better perspective on health.

As long as we stay on God's path, we will avoid many of life's difficulties. There was a time I took a few of my children for a walk near a park. The path was steep, but walkable. When we arrived at the top, and being in an adventurous mood, I suggested we go off the path and explore. At first we could make our way, but then we started running into thorny brambles. They were sharp and hard to avoid, and they would snagged our clothes and scratched our skin. In a similar way, God's path has been highlighted by His

---

[35] If you haven't repented from your own self-oriented living style and come to trust in Christ's work on the cross for your forgiveness of sin, then you still need to be saved. Christ welcomes us all to come to Him for salvation.

commands and wisdom.[36] In as much as we walk in His ways, we will avoid many snags and diseases.

Let's look at these holistic health instructions from the scriptures and see how they apply to new parents and the expecting Mom.

Marital relations during and after pregnancy

You might have a few questions like: What chance is there that I have a STD? If one of us has a STD, how will this affect the baby? Can we still have sex as usual during pregnancy? What about sex after birth?

1) Sexual diseases

> Let marriage be held in honor among all, and let the marriage bed be undefiled; for fornicators and adulterers God will judge (Heb 13:4).

STDs (sexually transmitted diseases) are ravishing the countries of the world. These diseases would all quickly disappear if men and women kept sexual intimacies between them and their spouse. Having sex out of wedlock with an impure partner is like playing Russian roulette. Disease can be avoided! We understand that some of these diseases have been transmitted via birth, but they are largely transmitted due to sexual immorality, therefore their name (STD).

110 million people in the United States alone are said to live with an incurable STD with an annual cost of 16 billion dollars.[37] This is more than one in three people! Other countries around the world

---

[36] We tend to fear His commands because we think that we will lose our freedoms. The fact is, living by His commandments means that we will gain our freedom. "Jesus therefore was saying to those Jews who had believed Him, If you abide in My word, then you are truly disciples of Mine; and you shall know the truth, and the truth shall make you free."(Jn 8:31-32).

[37] 2014 statistics from *"Hidden STD Epidemic: 110 Million Infections in the US"*. www.livescience.com/48100-sexually-transmitted-infections-50-states-map.html .

suffer similar problems. Women infected with STDs while pregnant can have premature rupture of the membranes, uterine infection, and early onset of labor. The latter can lead to a premature birth and possibly to infant death and disability.

What joy there is for a couple who lives under God's instructions on sexual purity! They have none of the extra pain, discomfort, fear, guilt, or expense. They can fully appreciate the joy of sexual intimacy, knowing deep in their heart that the world's diseases can't trouble them!

2) Abstinence for married couples too?

Sexual intercourse during pregnancy is fine. As the expecting mother's body changes, there will be some adjustments, but with a little extra love, sensitivity, and a good sense of humor, a couple's sexual life can be as great as ever. Some even suggest that sex helps bring along labor! But is there ever a need for abstinence? God's Word says there is.

Menstrual period abstinence
Also you shall not approach a woman to uncover her nakedness during her menstrual impurity (Lev 18:19).

We should first note that for those not yet expecting, God asks us to refrain from sex during a wife's menstrual period. If men have learned about self-control before marriage, this will remind them of that time. In fact, monthly abstinence does wonders for renewing the sexual relationship and the strengthening of self-control. It also helps eliminate or at least greatly lessen a woman's yeast infections.

Post-birth abstinence
When a woman gives birth and bears a male child… she shall remain in the blood of her purification for thirty-three days; she shall not touch any consecrated thing, nor enter the sanctuary, until the days of her purification are completed. …

> But if she bears a female child, ... she shall remain in the blood
> of her purification for sixty-six days.... This is the law for her
> who bears a child, whether a male or a female (Lev 12:2-5).

God even addresses the issue of post-birth abstinence. Women
were not to have sexual relations during menstruation. The above
instructions make a reference to the "blood", which infer
abstinence after birth. If we consider what our wives just went
through in delivering a child, abstinence makes sense. Their body
begins to change back to pre-pregnancy condition. Ligaments that
are loosened to accommodate the baby's birth begin to firm up.

Meanwhile, mothers are very busy caring for the new baby. They
need to learn or relearn how to nurse. Sometimes there is soreness.
They often simply lack the concentration that is needed for their
husband.[38]

God also uses this period of abstinence as a time to protect the wife
from getting pregnant again right away. God is clearly concerned
about the health of mother and newborn, and any future children.
Breast-feeding works as part of this 'birth-control' system by
inhibiting ovulation, but it only works when combined with the
above abstinence laws because it takes a few weeks after birth
before breastfeeding can inhibit ovulation. Many moms have been
surprised by another pregnancy soon after bearing a child. God
wants us to have strong families and healthy children. Note how
these laws protect the well-being of the new mother and works to
produce strong babies. God still loves weak babies, but we can all
agree with God's design in knowing that He wants our children to
thrive.

---

[38]I have yet to hear a reason for why this process takes two months for a girl and only one
month for a boy.

3) **Fertility and Infertility**

> But if you will truly obey his voice and do all that I say, then …
> shall be no one miscarrying or barren in your land; I will fulfill
> the number of your days (Ex 23:22, 26).

We have had our share of miscarriages. They are tragic. Not only
is the baby gone, but the mother's health could be in danger due to
severe bleeding. An expensive D&E (dilation and evacuation)
surgery is commonly recommended so that no remaining pieces
are left to cause infection or excessive bleeding. With each
miscarriage experience, we have sought more wisdom from God's
Word.

Living according to God's way brings the delivery of promises and
blessings. God is definitely pro-life; He wants married couples to
have children.

> You shall be blessed above all peoples; there shall be no male or
> female barren among you or among your cattle (Deut 7:14).

It is tragic, but in our sin-filled world, infertility happens. Infertility
is the result of a number of things: complications with certain
STDs like chlamydia and gonorrhea can increase infertility, and
certain chemical birth control methods like the pill confuse the
women's cycle, to name a few. Many women have found it is not
easy to get pregnant after being on the pill for a long time. Stress
from jobs or difficulties in relationships add to the causes of
infertility.

God wants His people to have many children. This is one way He
blesses us. One author astutely suggests that with all of the damage
that birth control devices cause, hasn't anyone realized that
multiple pregnancies is probably safer? God made the woman to
bear children. Uterine cancer is common only among women who

have not had children, and there are still more dangers for those who have held off until later to have children.[39]

Mary Pride reports that the regular use of birth control greatly increases the number of menstrual cycles a woman experiences and puts unhealthy stress on the reproductive organs, thus producing more uterine, breast, and cervical cancer.[40] Other kinds of birth control will diminish the woman's period. Each has its own side effects that must be taken in consideration when considering usage.[41]

God has made the man and woman to have sex throughout life without birth control except for the specified times of abstinence. God's ways should be trusted. Why are couples so eager to use birth control? Are they interfering with God's purpose? What does the world want? Why is its message so strong? Would you obey the world's message or God's?

> Behold, children are a gift of the LORD; The fruit of the womb is a reward (Ps 127:3).

Eating Habits and Nutrition

Everyone needs to pay attention to the food they are giving to their bodies, pregnant or nor, male or female. The expecting and nursing mothers have an urgent need to take care in how they treat and feed their bodies. Within minutes of a mother eating, children in utero will be affected. Usually this is good, but it can have negative side affects (things like dark green vegetables often causing gas in babies).

---

[39] The Way Home by Mary Pride (Crossway Books, 1985) pp. 51-52.

[40] Ibid, pp. 52-53.

[41] "What to Expect When You Go Off the Pill". www.huffingtonpost.com/2015/03/26/birth-control-side-effect_n_6911948.html

Through the Old Testament laws, God has spoken very clearly about things that can and cannot be eaten. It's worth it to consider whether God was not just interested in laws being obeyed but in strengthening the health of His people. There is no doubt that our modern society can more safely keep food with refrigeration and efficiently cook items, but we should be alert to God's concerns regarding diet for our children whether they are in or out of the womb.

1) Clean and Unclean

I've noted below a number of things that the Bible has listed as okay and not okay to eat. What I want you to take away from these passages isn't restriction, but rather the principle: not all animals are the same. In the Old Testament, the scavenger animals or bottom feeders were off limits because they eat from dead animals where disease reigns. Although pork is highly esteemed in some places, it is off limits. Adult hogs can carry over a dozen diseases that are transmissible to humans. They also carry parasites.

> These are the animals which you may eat: the ox, the sheep, the goat, the deer, the gazelle, the roebuck, the wild goat, the ibex, the antelope and the mountain sheep. And any animal that divides the hoof and has the hoof split in two and chews the cud, among the animals, that you may eat. Nevertheless, you are not to eat of these among those which chew the cud, or among those that divide the hoof in two... And the pig, because it divides the hoof but does not chew the cud, it is unclean for you. You shall not eat any of their flesh nor touch their carcasses. These you may eat of all that are in water: anything that has fins and scales you may eat, but anything that does not have fins and scales you shall not eat; it is unclean for you. You may eat any clean bird (Deut 14:3-11).

2) **Regarding blood-filled foods**

> Only you shall not eat the blood; you are to pour it out on the ground like water (Deut 12:16).

We should not eat things with blood in them. These days, the blood is typically drained from meats. This warning was given many times throughout the scriptures, even before the law, like to Noah after the flood. God simply explains that the life is in the blood.

3) **Breast milk for babies**

> To whom would He teach knowledge? And to whom would He interpret the message? Those just weaned from milk? Those just taken from the breast? (Is 28:9).

Moms should by all means breast feed their babies if at all possible. This is God's way! This, perhaps, does not need to be so stressed nowadays, but not too long ago very few mothers nursed their babies because they thought formula was more nutritious. One good example of God's excellent design of nursing is the presence of colostrum that is passed on to the baby in the first few days after birth. Being rich in protein and antibodies, the baby is protected from the diseases the mother has built up immunity to. The easy availability of formulas makes it easy to skip nursing and get back to one's daily activities. Baby formulas with all their ads "such and such added" encourage the mother to make inferior choices, instead of going through the process of learning how to breastfeed.

Although formula is good for emergencies, they are certainly far inferior to a mother's milk. We applaud those mothers who pump milk to give their children the best protective nutrients that breast milk supplies. Even better for the child would be a mother at home without the stress of busy schedules accompanied by a closer and softer touch. Moms produce lots of milk only when they are not stressed. Better to change one's lifestyle back to God's design at home.

4) Eating moderately and fasting

Some diseases occur simply because people eat too much. Obesity is a great killer. The digestive system is not easily able to handle large amounts of food. The scriptures teach us not only what we should and should not eat but also about how much we should eat.

> Do not be with heavy drinkers of wine, or with gluttonous eaters of meat (Pr 23:20).

> But you, when you fast, anoint your head, and wash your face so that you may not be seen fasting by men, but by your Father who is in secret; and your Father who sees in secret will repay you (Mat 6:17-18).

On the other hand, the Bible does teach us to fast. Fasting has both spiritual and physical benefits. On the physical side, fasting allows the body to use up stored fats and enables the system to properly cleanse itself. Expecting and nursing mothers are not expected to fast. One exception to this is for the mother that has a lot of morning sickness or all-day nausea. The nausea may be the body trying to rid itself of toxins. Fasting helps this process along. As the pregnancy progresses, it may be harder to eat regular-sized meals. It is important to be well nourished, so eating several smaller meals is an alternative.

5) Sugars and a sweet tooth

> It is not good to eat much honey, nor is it glory to search out one's own glory (Pr 25:27).

Nutrition books tell us that honey and sugar are of the same constitution, though honey has some trace minerals. Now if we could only convince ourselves to listen to the scripture about the dangers of consuming too much!

Actually, part of the problem is that we don't realize how much sugar we are eating. Younger people seem to be less influenced by excess sugar (except through cavities and obesity) but as a person's age increases, the harm sugar has becomes more evident, and the build-up of extensive overdosage becomes apparent.

Fructose sweetener, commonly derived from corn, is the modern day 'honey.' It is a common sugar additive and disguised by its name. "… Fructose has been implicated in heart disease, elevated blood cholesterol levels, and blood clotting. Worst of all, fructose causes the white blood cells of the immune system to become sleepy and unable to defend against harmful foreign invaders."[42]

Let's note how sugars and sweeteners can ruin your health.

- Sugar can suppress the immune system.
- Sugar can upset the body's mineral balance.
- Sugar can cause hyperactivity, anxiety, concentration difficulties, and crankiness in children.
- Sugar contributes to a weakened defense against bacterial infection.
- Sugar interferes with absorption of calcium and magnesium.
- Sugar can weaken eyesight.
- Sugar can produce an acidic stomach.
- Sugar can promote tooth decay.
- Sugar can produce candidiasis (a yeast infection).
- Sugar can indirectly cause hemorrhoids.
- Sugar can contribute to osteoporosis.

---

[42] Lick the Sugar Habit by Nancy Appleton (Avery, 1996), p. 57.

• Sugar can cause depression.

• Sugar can cause hormonal imbalance.[43]

Pregnant and nursing mothers must be careful not to eat too much sugar.

6) Fiber

Now, if the Lord wanted us to be healthy, it would follow that He would provide good food, which He did in the provision of grains.

> Now may God give you of the dew of heaven, And of the fatness of the earth, And an abundance of grain and new wine (Gen 27:28).

You might say that you eat plenty of grains. You eat rice, bread, and noodles made from wheat. What you may not realize is that most nutrition has been stripped from the grain before it was turned into flour for bread, pasta, etc. Did you ever notice how white the rice or bread is? This is not normal. The fiber (outer coating) has been removed during the milling process.

Modern day diets lack fiber. Lack of fiber leads to increased constipation and diseases that evolve from such condition. This preference for white grains started with the upper classes many years ago because they alone could afford such refined flour (or rice). However, this is not the case anymore.[44] The end result is that many people are now suffering from rich man's diseases. Those who have no access to such refined products receive the fiber they need from whole grains as they were meant to and do not suffer from appendicitis or other digestive disorders.

---

[43] Ibid, pp. 68-72. This is only a partial list!

[44] How strange it is that brown flour (whole-wheat flour) is more expensive than heavily processed white flour!

Some might protest by pointing out that certain essential vitamins are added to bread products or breakfast cereals, but consider this: what about the other twenty essential vitamins and minerals that were stripped in the refinement process? Only a few vitamins can actually be replaced. See the chart in the sidebar.[45] God's original packaging of grains can't be beat. Fiber can be easily added to ones diet by eating whole grains, vegetables, and fruits with skin. Eating out less will give opportunity to prepare more healthy meals at home. Fortunately, information and access to gluten free foods, whole grains, has greatly increased in the last decade. But the challenge to take time to cook still remains before us!

What do we do?

- We started out by buying whole grain flour and making our own bread in bread machines.

- Later we learned that more than 50% of the nutrients were lost within 24 hours after grinding the grain. Even our whole-wheat flour was lacking. So we looked into buying our own grains and a home grinder. This saved us a lot of money. Grains are cheap and easy to store (if in colder climate). Best of all, we got a nicer flour, lots of fresh nutrients, and many grain choices (kamut, rice, soy beans, rye, corn, etc.) to

Whole Wheat Flour Nutrients	Nutrients Loss in White Flour
thiamine (B-1)	77%
riboflavin (B-2)	67%
niacin (B-3)	81%
pyridoxine (B-6)	72%
choline	30%
folic acid	67%
pantothenic acid	50%
vitamin E	86%
chromium	40%
manganese	86%
selenium	16%
zinc	98%
iron	75%
cobalt	89%
calcium	60%
sodium	78%
potassium	77%
magnesium	85%
phosphorus	91%
molybdenum	48%
copper	68%
fiber	89%

add to the wheat when making flour for bread or other things

---

[45] Adapted from <u>More than Breakfast</u> by Sue Gregg (Eating Better Cookbooks, 1993), p. 53.

like pizza. A soft winter wheat (pastry flour) is better for cakes.

- When our family outgrew 1 or 2 loaves a day, we switched from a bread machine to making it ourselves. With powerful dough mixers, the process was easy and quick.

- We also began to use more brown rice, and added oatmeal to different dishes. Our children are now quite accustomed to 100% brown rice, though previously we mixed about half brown and half white.

Let me say that eating right really brings many unthought of help to our families. Yes, we as a family do eat pork, but we make sure it is cooked well. We are not bound to the Old Testament laws, but it should remind us that God understands problems of disease that plague good health. Modern society with its instant meals has brought trouble into many families through poor nutrition.

Other Health Concerns

There are a number of other issues that are closely connected to our nutritional health.

1) Rest and sleep

Remember the sabbath day, to keep it holy. Six days you shall labor and do all your work, but the seventh day is a sabbath of the LORD your God; in it you shall not do any work, you or your son or your daughter, your male or your female servant or your cattle or your sojourner who stays with you. For in six days the LORD made the heavens and the earth, the sea and all that is in them, and rested on the seventh day; therefore the LORD blessed the sabbath day and made it holy (Ex 20:8-11).

This law, to keep one day for rest, relaxation, and spiritual worship is largely ignored in our modern lifestyles. We need to keep in mind that constant work equals constant stress. If we do not take a day for rest and recuperation, we will find ourselves living for work instead of working for a living. Do you actually pause one day each week and worship God or do you compromise?

The expectant mother will face all sorts of sleeping challenges. That is fine. Take an extra nap or three. Taking naps is not wasting time, but caring for your body and the baby. During pregnancy, waking up at night to go to the bathroom a couple times can be a drain on your daytime energy, but you can think of it as good training for the times when the baby wakes for feeding after birth.

Sleep is important for all. It's been found that entertainment, including televisions, movies, computer games, etc. all act as stimulants. Physical stimuli like caffeine and sugar (like late night ice cream) keeps people up later as well. Cut these things out so that you can see if you are missing out on your body's sleep signals.

2) Contagious diseases

Our society is still willing to be foolish about dealing with contagious diseases like STDs, including HIV, but otherwise they seem to be getting much more biblical on how to respond to such diseases. We just need a few serious flus or viruses to go around to keep us alert. We appreciate the Bible's instructions on how isolation coupled with careful detection can help protect us.

> But if the priest looks at it, and behold, there are no white hairs in it and it is not lower than the skin and is faded, then the priest shall isolate him for seven days (Lev 13:21).

It is a major step for governments to actually restrain a person's freedom because of the disease he has. God told us long ago, as much as we don't like to hear it, that isolation works. The Lord thinks it so important that He spent a whole chapter (Leviticus 13) on how to detect and treat certain conditions.

Isolation is an important principle for parents of little children to keep in mind. What a terrible habit people have in touching the hands of our infants and children! Parents need to learn to keep our children away from sick children as much as possible. Of course, there will be times when this is impossible. We will need to pray and watch so that we can learn more. Mothers need to wash their hands often and train their children to do likewise.

3) Circumcision

There is ongoing debate on the advantages and disadvantages of circumcising our sons. We will not go into the details here, but I'll mention two advantages of circumcision here:

- The statistics show that cervical cancer is rare among Jewish and Muslim women.
- Circumcised boys and men are cleaner and freer from common infections than the uncircumcised boys and men.

And when eight days were completed before His circumcision, His name was then called Jesus, the name given by the angel before He was conceived in the womb (Lu 2:21).

Those who espouse non-circumcision are mostly concerned about the pain and possible loss of pleasure. God knows that the benefit of circumcision outweighs the pain, which is forgotten.

Very interestingly, vitamin K, which causes blood to clot, is absent until day eight; on the eighth day, the day boys are to be circumcised, the blood clotting chemical prothrombin skyrockets to higher than normal levels (110%).[46]

4) Stimulants and drugs

For the heavy drinker and the glutton will come to poverty, And drowsiness will clothe a man with rags (Prov 23:21).

---

[46] None of these Diseases, p. 22.

Drugs of all sorts pervade our lives. They negatively affect babies, while they're in the womb or nursing, whether it be cocaine (and other illicit drugs), caffeine (coffee, tea, chocolate, soda), or nicotine (smoking). Pregnant and nursing mothers must take caution when it comes to deciding what to eat. If they wouldn't give it to their child directly, then they shouldn't give it indirectly either.

It is best to think of medicines, even over-the-counter ones, as drugs so that we handle them more carefully. Many people are concerned that the overuse of antibiotics can cause long-term harm to a child's immune system. We need to do a better job of seriously paying attention to the side effects and how they affect the kids. The industry has been doing a better job in informing us of possible dangers, but they are hardly perfect, and we must be responsible for ourselves.

Relational Diseases

The Lord says a good deal about problems that develop from improperly dealing with people and problems. As our Maker, God knows exactly how to handle each situation in which we might find ourselves. Jesus modeled this principled problem-solving for us.

Let's look at a few injunctions that will protect us from falling into the trap of ignoring unsolved issues. The event of pregnancy and birth might distract us from relational problems, but it does not solve them. If not purposely identified and solved, they will become our children's problems. God seriously warned succeeding generations, "Visiting the iniquity of the fathers on the children, on the third and the fourth generations of those who hate Me" (Ex 20:5).

1) Forgive or be not forgiven

An unforgiving spirit generates a whole set of physical, emotional and spiritual problems. A doctor once said, "Your blood pressure is up today." With a smile the patient answered, "I can easily account for that. I just had a heated argument with another patient in your waiting room."[47]

> He who conceals his transgressions will not prosper, But he who confesses and forsakes them will find compassion (Pr 28:13).

> Then Peter came and said to Him, "Lord, how often shall my brother sin against me and I forgive him? Up to seven times?" Jesus said to him, "I do not say to you, up to seven times, but up to seventy times seven (Matt 18:21-22).

There are many studies linking heart disease and bitterness.[48] If we, as parents, do not forgive others of their sins, then we are going to bring harm to our children. We are responsible to set an example of right behavior. If we tell our children that we all must love one another but they don't see us modeling it, why should they take our teaching seriously? We must come to the cross and forgive others, and in some situations, we must repent for not quickly extending forgiveness. Jesus tells us to forgive seventy times seven. If not, bitterness will pile up in our heart, causing all sorts of abnormalities. Is there anyone you need to forgive for offending you?

2) Fears & Worries

Fear and worry devastate people's lives in similar ways. God's answer is to fear only Him, and to trust Him in our every

---

[47] None of these Diseases. pp. 71-72.

[48] "Rein In the Rage: Anger and Heart Disease". www.webmd.com/heart-disease/features/rein-in-rage-anger-heart-disease

circumstance.[49] When we obey God, we can trust Him and eliminate fear and worry.

> Do not be anxious then, saying, 'What shall we eat?' or 'What shall we drink?' or 'With what shall we clothe ourselves? (Mat 6:31)

> O my God, in Thee I trust, Do not let me be ashamed; Do not let my enemies exult over me (Ps 25:2).

> Trust in Him at all times, O people; Pour out your heart before Him; God is a refuge for us. [Selah.] (Ps 62:8).

We quickly gather from these passages that we don't need to lose our sleep or health because of our fears and worries. Let me give you a brief story on how one famous man found peace of heart. J.C. Penney's business was solid during the 1929 crash, but he had made some unwise personal investments. He became so worried that he couldn't sleep. The pain from his shingles was so extreme that he was hospitalized and given sedatives. One night he even thought he might die. He wrote death notes to his loved ones, but something happened the next morning that changed his life.

The great business tycoon heard singing in the hospital chapel. He struggled to go listen and as he entered the chapel, the group was singing, "God will Take Care of You" followed by scripture and a prayer. In response, Mr. Penney wrote,

> Suddenly something happened. I can't explain it. I can only call it a miracle. I felt as if I had been instantly lifted out of the darkness of a dungeon into warm, brilliant sunlight. I felt as if I had been transported from hell to paradise. I felt the power of God as I had never felt it before. I realized then that I alone was responsible for all my troubles. I know that God with His love was there to help me. From that day to this, my life has

---

[49] Check out www.foundationsforfreedom.net/Help/Store/Intros/ Overcome_Anxiety.html for my book, *Overcoming Anxiety: Finding Peace, Discovering God.*

been free from worry. I am seventy-one years old, and the most dramatic and glorious minutes of my life were those I spent in that chapel that morning: 'God will take Care of You.'[50]

God has a greater plan for each of our lives than we could ever plan for ourselves. The fears and worries that we retain as parents will be passed down to our children. They learn from us, the good and the bad. How? Worries and fears are built on doubts about God's ability to care for us. Instead of passing on faith to trust God, we actually pass on doubt! Are there any worries or fears in your life? Are there circumstances that cause worry or fear to rise in your heart? Learn to trust God in those tenuous situations, and replace worry with trust.

3) Love or selfishness

In our family devotional times, we sing a song with the line, "Love is something if you give it away." Our families must be filled with love. Critical remarks, negative attitudes, and harsh and unkind words all work to destroy our children. Unless we get rid of our bitterness, judgmental attitudes, pride, jealousy, and hatred, our bodies will suffer right along with our children. Haven't you seen how families can be destroyed by a critical spirit?

God's solution is free. It only calls for a commitment to keep giving away the very best. As we do, God will keep filling the bins of our hearts with more and more. Grudges, vendettas, scheming, and plots all have to be pushed out of our lives.

For the whole Law is fulfilled in one word, in the statement, "You shall love your neighbor as yourself" (Gal 5:14).

---

[50] None of these Diseases., p. 98.

Summary

God's way is the best way! All we need to do to discover this is go back to His Word. In it, we will find solutions for everything from limiting sugar intake to worry. God speaks directly about sex, good hygiene, what to eat, and what not to eat. God has linked good health with obedience. If we can understand and follow God's designs, none of the diseases of the world will come upon us (Ex 15:26). We will live long lives (Ex 20:12).

We should be humbled by the words God speaks later in Deuteronomy 28 where He tells His people what will happen if they do not obey Him. Remember, blessings do not come automatically. They are contingent on obedience.

> And He will bring back on you all the diseases of Egypt of which you were afraid, and they shall cling to you. Also every sickness and every plague which, not written in this book of this law, the Lord will bring on you until you are destroyed (Deut 28:60-61).

God is passionate about His people's health. We certainly need to seek Him and His ways if we are to have excellent health. Furthermore, as we follow the guidelines that God has set for us, we will be more capable of giving loving and healthy lives to our children. In the end, we can say to our children that this all is God's gift to you from us. Parents play a huge role in establishing healthy children that fear the Lord.

#3 Study Questions

1. How do we know that God is concerned with our health?

2. What discoveries are attributed to Dr. Semmelweis?

3. What are the benefits of God's Family Health Plan?

4. What does it cost?

5. Can STDs (sexually transmitted diseases) be avoided? If so, how?

6. Name one thing the Bible says about abstinence for married couples.

7. How much effort should a new mom make to breastfeed her baby?

8. What is one advantage to fasting?

9. List four problems that heavy sugar use can cause.

10. Why is daily fiber intake so important?

11. Why isn't eating bread good enough to get your daily fiber quota?

12. What important medical procedure do we get from Leviticus 13:21?

13. What is one way an unforgiving heart can affect our child?

Preparations for Childbirth

Making preparations for the arrival of your baby is one of the most thrilling experiences in life. We love to see the proud joy of parents when they cuddle their new little one. Before the child arrives, though, there's a lot to do. The parents-to-be will be highly motivated to make everything just right.

Many parents, though, look back to find that they were rather unprepared for what really happened during childbirth. Making it worse, many of these parents live far from their own parents, which limits immediate support. New parents are largely uninformed about the childbirth process and the various hospital procedures that take place before, during, and after birth, which makes it hard to make wise decisions. This lack of preparation occurs, in part, from never having experienced childbirth, but new interventions and procedures, thanks to modern medicine, make it extra hard. Fortunately, many classes that provide further advice are now widely offered.

This chapter will shed some light on the situations parents might face and the urgent decisions that often need to be made during the childbirth process. We hope that with the knowledge and encouragement in this chapter, parents will be able to make decisions informed by trust in the God who created this marvelous process. Decisions that are best suited to your specific situation are extremely important. We recognize that we are not the last resource on these subjects; we are not doctors. We are simply the parents of eight children, who are eager to share the wisdom that we have gleaned from the experience of raising them. We desire to present a God-centered perspective of childbirth, which is a perspective that is so often ignored in the pregnancy books that line your local bookstores. As you read on, mark areas that you want to learn more about. Hopefully, you will find time to research it now before having your baby.[51]

The Joy of Having a Baby

The most obvious fruit of marriage is children. God has designed DNA in such a way that a child will reflect both parents. The DNA of the father and mother combine to make a whole new person; DNA from both a father *and* mother is essential. A question that family and friends often asked after birth is, "Who does he/she look most like?" A child is a miracle of life from God, and every child is made in the image of God, and therefore must be protected as a unique, important creation. Each child beautifully reflects the parents' oneness and is an embodiment of their union.

David the Psalmist penned the following words from Psalm 139:13-16 under the inspiration of the Holy Spirit.

---

[51] Unfortunately, we cannot recommend any one book. We suggest buying several so to protect you from any bias that the one author might have. Make sure one book emphasizes the 'natural' birth, but be careful in your choices.

> **Psalm 139:13-16**
> For You formed my inward parts; You wove me in my mother's womb. I will give thanks to You, for I am fearfully and wonderfully made; Wonderful are Your works, And my soul knows it very well. My frame was not hidden from You, When I was made in secret, *And* skillfully wrought in the depths of the earth; Your eyes have seen my unformed substance; And in Your book were all written The days that were ordained *for me,* When as yet there was not one of them.

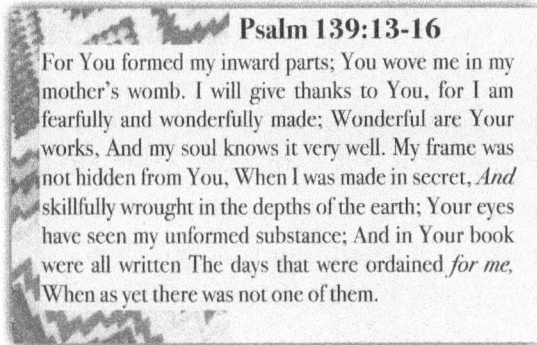

Wrapped into these few sentences, are strong assertions about every person:

- God formed our inward parts.
- God weaves each person together.
- Each child is "fearfully and wonderfully made."
- God plans our days; they are ordained for us even before they happen.

Not one of us is an accident from God's point of view, and so we should consider each child from this perspective.[52] We might not have planned for the child, but God sure did!

Unexpected Happenings

When first discovering conception, parents are usually eager to tell everyone, and of course they have the right and freedom to do so. They should be aware, however, that miscarriages happen more often than they might think. Mothers who have had miscarriages in the past are much more reluctant to share the news of a new pregnancy with others because they will be more cautious and will prepare themselves emotionally in case the new child also meets a untimely end.

---

[52] Some children have thought themselves as unwanted because they were unplanned. They may think they are less loved. We can help such people understand that maybe their parents did not plan for them, or even want them, but God did!

It is often harder for mothers to handle a miscarriage than fathers, both physically and emotionally, because they, after all, have carried the baby and connected with him or her. Miscarriages happen more often at a very early stage. Any odd bleeding should be reported to the doctor. The wife should also be concerned with any bleeding any time during pregnancy. Often, it doesn't mean anything is wrong, but it's better to be safe than sorry. There may be times that the doctor might need to give special advice. In some cases there isn't much to be done.

Life and death never happens by accident, they remain under God's sovereign control. The more we have confidence in these truths, the easier it is to adjust to the loss of a little one. The longer the child lived, the harder it will be to understand why the child's life was not extended. We should not expect to find answers for the "Why?" questions we have, but we can find comfort in God's providential wisdom and love.

David had one child out of wedlock and was extremely anxious for the life of that child. When those around him discovered that the baby was dead, they were afraid to tell David over fear of what he might do to himself, largely because he had already been fasting and crying out to God on behalf of this child.

> Then it happened on the seventh day that the child died. And the servants of David were afraid to tell him that the child was dead, for they said, "Behold, while the child was still alive, we spoke to him and he did not listen to our voice. How then can we tell him that the child is dead, since he might do himself harm!" But when David saw that his servants were whispering together, David perceived that the child was dead; so David said to his servants, "Is the child dead?" And they said, "He is dead." So David arose from the ground, washed, anointed himself, and changed his clothes; and he came into the house of the LORD and worshiped (2 Sam 12:18-20).

Interestingly, once he discovered the
baby was dead, he put on his regular
garments and resumed life as usual.
We see in the Psalms that King
David had tremendous trust in God.
This trust was not shaken in bad
times. David's pleas were only for grace in the time of deserved
judgment.

Parents need to have the same unwavering respect and trust in
God's purposes for the children He calls us to raise and love. The
baby, whether in the womb, two months old, or 18 years old,
belongs to God. God issued life. True, He created this new human
being through the parents, but God is still ultimately responsible for
the child. The parents are only stewards.

The concept of stewardship will serve parents well if they can
remember it through the long years of childrearing. It will help
them do their best to care for the child by feeding, caring, helping,
protecting, and training. Most of all, they'll see the importance of
introducing their child to God and providing a godly upbringing.
The concept of stewardship reminds parents that they have limited
resources; they cannot heal their child, nor can they protect him or
her completely. They won't be able to fix all their child's problems
either.

This is true with every aspect of a child's needs. Parents desire so
much for their child–like the ability to learn quickly, more
accurately, and more diligently. Parents often experience pride in
their child's early accomplishments: 'Oh, he started walking early'
or 'She is already talking.' They must remember that the child, in
the end, is God's. God has woven all sorts of gifts and desires
together, and has designed a special destiny for each child. Some

children live short lives while others don't even hold on to their life past the womb.[53]

It is good and needy, therefore, to acknowledge both God's part in the life of the child as well as your part. This can be done through a simple prayer even before the baby is born. Through our simple but honest words, we must place our dependence upon God for the wisdom, resources, and love needed to raise that child. And indeed, if anything discouraging happens, we can trust God in His sovereign will. Because of our sin, we all must die, some earlier than others, but all must die. Here is a sample prayer:

> Dear Father in Heaven, we come to dedicate this child you have brought into the world through us. We are glad. We are excited. And yet we want to recognize that you are the Sovereign Creator of this child's life. All of his or her special needs are in your hands. Please watch over this child. You know our heart's desire.

> We desire that this child grow to be a godly man or woman who serves you and brings glory to your Name. Take these desires, dear Lord. We entrust them to you. If you in your sovereign purpose decide to create the child with a disability or giftedness, short days or long, ugliness or beauty, let it be known that we will trust you just the same. This child is yours. We entrust this child to you. Help us watch over this child as you would desire. Keep him or her close to you, O Lord. Forever yours in Christ, –the parents.

---

[53] Parents with children who have died early often ask the question about the salvation of their children. If we stick close to the scriptures, there are two ruling teachings. 1) All are naturally dead in Adam- all have a sin nature. But children so young, of course, have not had time to express their sin nature. 2) God condemns those who are in Adam.

 I like to keep an open door for God to work special things in a child's life before birth such as in John the Baptist and Jeremiah. But these cases seem more rare. In summary, we need to put hope away for those aborted children. But do remember that their judgment will be just. God is wise.

Through this prayer, you are acknowledging and committing yourself to certain important truths. Most central is that the child is God's, and as a result of that, He has every right to do as He wants with each child. Lastly, you are acknowledging that you are His steward and that you need His help to watch over your child.

> Can I not, O house of Israel, deal with you as this potter does?" declares the LORD. "Behold, like the clay in the potter's hand, so are you in My hand, O house of Israel" (Jer 18:6).

Baby Preparations

The great thing about birth is that God has taken care of all the details. It might not seem that way, what with all the doctor appointments and things to read and plan, but it is true. Near the end of a pregnancy, a burst of energy occurs that helps the mother-to-be make sure everything is ready for the baby. I love to see the whole cycle take place. The wife can rest only when she has everything in place and the needed items in hand.

There is no need for us to go into what is needed for the birth here since wherever you choose to have the child will see to it that you get such a list. Only remember that it's important to gather the items by 37-38 weeks so that nothing is left to the last second! Babies do sometimes come earlier than expected!

The baby's room needs to be clean and protected from cold drafts and bugs as much as possible. Designer furniture is not necessary to raise a happy, healthy child. Don't let the ads fool you or make you feel ashamed if you cannot afford the best furniture in the world. After all, if God our Father was willing to have His Son sleep in a manger (food trough for animals), surely we cannot feel ashamed in not having top-of-the-line furniture.

And this will be a sign for you: you will find a baby wrapped in cloths, and lying in a manger (Luke 2:12).

Lavish treatment and giving our child everything money can buy will surely lead the child to think that he should be served rather than learning how to serve.

Knowledge-Based birth

The level of involvement that doctors have in the birth process is a more recent development in society. For many thousands of years, women assisted other women in giving birth. Some of the modern techniques are in fact unnecessary and hurtful, while others are helpful, and some are even critical to saving a baby's life in certain circumstances. Perhaps if there was help (now termed 'intervention') for Rachel when she was giving birth to Benjamin, she may not have died. These interventions are for the expectant mother, but every one of them has an effect on the baby.

Modern culture has accepted the 'medicalization' of childbirth over the last one hundred years. Even in the early 1900s, most children were born at home. Childbirth was natural and normal. God designed it to be a normal process, much like bowel movements or puberty. The only thing needed was for someone to catch the baby coming out! Of course, this is bit of an exaggeration, but we often find ourselves hurting for the mothers who are burdened by the medical safeguards. For example, mothers are typically required to lie down once they enter the labor ward so that a device can monitor the baby. But laying down goes contrary to God's use of gravity to bring about speedier labors.

We have had a good deal of experience with midwives and are very thankful for them. They are willing to give you time, explanations, and education regarding your choices and the implications of those choices. Midwives are skilled and gifted in the knowledge of birth techniques and after-birth care.

We might wonder whether all the modern interventions are really helpful or necessary. Are sonograms (prenatal ultrasounds) necessary? Not usually. Is there any harm? There are many studies out there showing their safety[54], and yet people are still raising questions of their routine use.[55] Midwives use a handheld Doppler that detects the heartbeat. High-risk mothers benefit greatly by a more careful watch provided by an ultrasound. Eating well and getting plenty of rest and exercise go a long way to making a healthy baby.

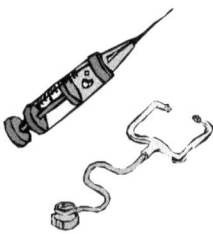

Hearing a new child's heartbeat at ten weeks gestation is a thrilling experience for parents. Checkups should be just that: making sure nothing is wrong. We can trust God's design of the childbirth process, especially when the mother is faithful to eat balanced meals, govern her weight gain/loss, and ingest good levels of iron. Of course, those with significant health problems, who are considered 'high risk', need to take additional precautions.

People are responsible to make wise and very expensive decisions for themselves, but they often lack the knowledge and expertise on certain matters that would allow them to make those decisions properly. Doctors, on the other hand, have this knowledge and expertise, but generally do not take the needed time with their patients to explain everything. Good doctors are unable to spend the time they would like with their patients due to hospital, insurance, and financial constraints.

---

[54] "Ultrasound Imaging". www.fda.gov/Radiation-EmittingProducts/RadiationEmittingProductsandProcedures/MedicalImaging/ucm115357.htm

[55] "Ultrasound: More Harm than Good?" www.midwiferytoday.com/articles/ultrasoundwagner.asp

In an ideal world, doctors would be able to spend more time with parents-to-be so that they could have all the needed information by which they could make wise decisions. But unfortunately, this world is not ideal, and parents-to-be are often fearful because they know that they do not have all the information they need to make good decisions, and it's unrealistic to think that parents can learn everything that a doctor would know.

In the end, we suggest that you find a doctor who will take the time to explain things, who has common values, and who will not be offended if you consider different choices than he suggests. Doctors are invaluable for their knowledge, so we need to choose a good doctor so that we can make godly and healthy decisions for our lives. Let's continue by learning more about a number of specific areas of need.

Is there any cure for nausea or morning sickness?

Nausea is a common sign of pregnancy and affects some mothers-to-be more than others. We still don't know of any sure-fire solutions for pregnancy-related nausea. You've probably heard a million suggestions: eat crackers before getting up in the morning, sour plums or ginger candies, don't get fatigued, etc., but there are probably as many solutions as there are women.

My wife accepted that she was going to feel nauseous for a time and did her best getting on with life. One suggestion we incorporated into our lives was fasting. Nausea is usually the body trying to rid itself of toxins. We heard that fasting with just fresh juice for a couple of days may have some benefit. But as with anything medical, check with your doctor before trying anything radical.

Linda has suffered a lot of nausea. During her first pregnancy, she even needed to quit her job due to the intensity of the nausea.

Because I was still in university, we had to make a lot of life adjustments to receive God's gift of our first precious child. God is always interested in shaping our family experiences to create an ongoing appreciation of His grace. We still praise God for the many ways He provided for us financially during that time. Actually, we sought out a midwife for the birth of our first child because I was in college without coverage. Unbeknown to us, this choice would become a great blessing to our family through the years.

What blood tests and other tests need to be done?

The mother will be expected to have a number of blood tests, but not all are necessary. The government has rules, and doctors and midwives have their own preferences beyond those. Often the parents can choose to forego them if they are knowledgeable about the test. In most cases, mothers do not have a clue as to what is being given to them, and doctors rarely spend much time with them explaining. This is one reason we enjoyed the time to talk during checkups with our midwives.

Midwives believe knowledge is important in order to make the right decisions. In most cases, doctors are willing to bypass discussions because they expect the patient to obey rather than learn. This is where medical knowledge can be more crippling than helpful. Less intervention is only possible if we gain knowledge, increase our understanding by frank discussion, and have confidence in what we know and decide. This will enable us to hold to our decisions when we're challenged. The doctor should honor the parents' decision and not just tolerate it. If you sense an unwillingness to discuss or a lean to bypass a regular procedure, you might consider changing your doctor. Midwives have a track record of being very willing to help parents make the right choices.

Here is an example of this tension. What do you say when the doctor suggests a test for birth defects? The doctors and nurses can exert quite a bit of pressure. They often do not spend the time telling you of the possible dangers of these tests or their possible psychological effects upon your life. Nor do they explain what a parent is to do with the knowledge. It's a good rule of thumb to ask: "Why is this test necessary?" "What difference will it make in my treatment?"

At the initial check-up, the doctor should order several blood tests: blood type, RH factor, red blood cell count, a test for gonorrhea, and probably some others. Also expect to have a urinalysis. At every check-up, you may have your urine checked for protein and glucose. The doctor or midwife will check on the position of the baby, especially in the last trimester. They will check your weight to see if there is excessive swelling, and should inquire about any discomforts or problems you may be having.

Every doctor or midwife will operate from a given set of assumptions. They assume that you'd want to know if anything was wrong. Some people would want to abort a child with a defect and try again. If the results of a test will not change your decision, then why should you have the test done in the first place? Is it worth the risks?

If you have the test and it comes out showing that the child is defective, this gives them even more cause to give you pressure to follow through with an abortion. Unfortunately, too many people, including some doctors, believe there are too many people on this earth and so have no moral problem with limiting the earth's population. This is exactly what new parents do *not* need. We have heard several real stories about parents who have trusted God with what was expected to be a deformed or defected child, yet things were just fine.[56] The birth defect test is not always accurate; instead of trusting a sometimes defective test, we ought to trust our perfect God. If God wants to take the life of our child, then let God do it. We should be on a mission to preserve life.

You, whether a parent or not, are responsible for your decisions. Unfortunately, health insurance has blurred this sense of personal responsibility. When an individual has to pay for each item or procedure, then he will be much more concerned about whether or not each procedure needs to be done and the reason why. Who wants to pay for something unnecessary? When it is free, people are more open to subjecting themselves to tests without first questioning them.

In conclusion, many parents-to-be just do not have any insight into the real problems. There are many very kind and gracious doctors. Find them and use them.

Where have all the midwives gone?

Years ago, midwives did virtually all the deliveries, and for a while in 'modern' countries, it even became popular to have a doctor come to do a home birth. Then, doctors stopped making house calls and the mothers had to go to the hospital. Up until that point, the hospital was for sick people with diseases. The mothers were, and still are, concerned about giving birth in such disease-ridden, unfriendly places like hospitals, but they have been willing to make that change, thinking that it must be safer to be in a hospital near doctors and emergency medical equipment.

---

[56] Doesn't God love children with defects too? Of course! We are not God, and so we must trust God for these children. We are stewards of God's creation.

Labor

For a while, the practice of midwifery was almost stamped out, but over the last three decades, it has made a comeback. Midwives have to work with doctors and hospitals that are favorable, or at least tolerable, to their work; if a mother-to-be develops a condition outside of the midwife's expertise[57], she'll need to use the hospital and doctors available there. The nice thing is that the midwife still often delivers the baby or at least accompanies the mom in the hospital.

Fortunately, in most births, there are no problems. Baby after baby get high APGAR scores.[58] The less intervention with anesthesia and monitors, the better the outcome. Maybe we should note here again that we are not saying it is wrong or immoral to use anesthesia or monitors because some situations warrant these interventions. However, we must believe that God's natural way works best in most cases. Trust God with all the pain, discomforts, odd feelings, etc. The mother's intuition will take over and she need only work with it. It is often the blank of the unknown that causes fear—fear of whether you will be able to deliver, fear of whether you will have to have a C-section, fear of whether something will be wrong with your child. Trust God to be your strength and His

---

[57] Many problems derive from poor health. Keeping physically fit is important. Think of it as getting ready for a competitive event where you need all your muscles in good working order. Sex is fine. Regular walks and moderate exercise is important. Plan naps, but otherwise keep up with routine.

[58] APGAR is a one and five minute test after the birth of the baby. The baby's heart rate, respiratory effort, color, reflex, and muscle tone are simple observed and scored.

design is best. Please do not use meditative techniques stemming from Eastern religions, but instead concentrate, if you can, on how God is working with you to bring new life into this world. The intensity of contractions will ebb and flow, depending on the length of the labor. Husbands that are present can certainly act as coaches; between contractions, try talking about humorous past events, or even in less intense times be praying, going over names for the baby, reflecting on some comforting Bible verses, or anything else that might be helpful.

When has true labor started?

If someone found an accurate way to predict a baby's birth, they would make millions of dollars. How many times has a woman come in with all the signs of soon having a baby, but instead of delivering, the labor pains slow down and then stop?

Longer labor

We have had our share of false labors. Through the years, we developed a better understanding of the real signs, but honestly, who wants to wait at home during contractions that last from twenty to sixty seconds, every 4-5 minutes, for over half an hour? There is a very real chance the mother could go into transition very quickly and deliver. A pelvic exam will tell how far the mother has dilated. Sometimes a mother dilates to 3 centimeters and stops. If the water breaks, then she will need to go in. Delivery should happen within 24 hours of the water breaking to avoid infection.

We have had several close calls! With our oldest son, Linda walked into the midwives birthing center and went straight to the bathroom. Her water broke as soon as she sat on the toilet. He was born within 15 minutes of entering the door of the midwife center. With our second child, I still remember the doctor running down the hall in his t-shirt and shorts, not having any time to properly dress. He barely had time to catch the baby! Good

thing, too, because I was not much use–outside the door half laying down and about to faint!

Linda's last birth was a planned home birth. The midwives that we had used throughout the years had no birth center for a couple years, so we chose birth at home. All the kids were at home, and a few in the birth room. It was a great family experience. The midwife was trying to get there in time. I was trying to remember the instructions in case the midwife couldn't make it, but fortunately they had cell phones so, if necessary, they could lead me through step-by-step. This didn't comfort me much, though I no longer got faintish near birth.

Thankfully, the midwife was there well before baby Rebekah arrived. I was relieved. She brought in a few bags of equipment, including an oxygen tank in case of an emergency. Linda chose to squat to give birth, and out came the baby, first the head and then the body with a rush. With towels and cloths, the mess wasn't too bad (this was my biggest concern). Mom was happy. Gram was delighted. The baby was beautiful. Our family was happy, and Mom could go to sleep in her own bed!

We share stories of close calls and births in odd places, but usually the timing works out fine. It is comforting to have phones to get in contact with the doctor or midwife if necessary on the way to give birth. The tradeoff is that if it isn't real labor that persists and leads to birth, the parents can feel rather awkward going home again. At least you will have another try!

Does a woman always need to be shaved?

For a while, part of giving birth in a hospital meant that a mother needed to be shaved. This was supposedly done for hygienic reasons, but today there are more options for mothers in hospitals! It is also nice to see the more friendly maternity wards. Hopefully, midwives will again be fully accepted by the medical community and be part of the hospitals. This is changing for the better now that some hospitals even have their own birthing center and midwives.

Do they need anesthesia?

Women do not *need* anesthesia, at least not in most cases. In fact, anesthetics can make it harder for the mother to push. C-sections sometimes occur because the Mom can't push. At the same time, the doctor and the hospital get more money out of a caesarean. Anesthetics will pass to the baby very quickly, which can make the baby very sleepy and unable to latch on to nurse. Epidural anesthesia are considered safer and less intrusive than general anesthesia, though one should read up on the pros and cons before labor.

Hospital staff can't give much support to the mother to enable her to endure through the whole process. Without this coaching, it can be difficult, especially in the case of an inexperienced mother. Another pro for use of a midwife is that she is with you the whole time. They back off if they aren't needed, but are right there explaining everything when necessary.

Shall I bring to the point of birth, and not give delivery?" says the LORD. "Or shall I who gives delivery shut the womb?" says your God (Is 66:9).

Labor is intensive, but the joy of the new baby and thew release of certain chemicals in the body help the mother endure and quickly forget her labor pains. She needs support and proper positioning. Think of labor as pain with a joyous purpose—a new little life soon to be cradled in your arms! That new child is the visible result of your love and oneness with your spouse.

Is electronic fetal monitoring (EFM/IFM) necessary?

Electronic fetal monitoring is not necessary except in certain high-risk situations. Just look at the billions of safe births that have gone on without its use. There are plenty of other signs that enable the obstetrician or midwife to know if the baby is in distress. In fact, monitoring messes up the whole birth process by requiring the mother to lay down on her back (lithotomy). This monitor might be convenient in the case of an absent physician, but a laboring mother should not be pinned down on her back! The mother should be up and about as much as possible to allow gravity to expand the diameter of the cervix to ten centimeters so the child can be born safely.

Lying down is the worst thing for a mother in labor, even though it is the most common position in hospitals. She should be walking around as much as possible. We are not saying the Mom can't lie down or even take a quick nap if it is at all possible. But to be strapped to a bed by monitoring equipment is not helpful at all. We suggest you discuss this with your obstetrician ahead of time. We need to work with gravity's pull and strong un-anesthetized muscles if at all possible. Interventional equipment can actually prolong labor and make it more exhausting. This exhaustion in many cases forces the mothers to give up to the doctor's recommendation for a cesarean birth. A vaginal birth is much healthier for the Mom and the baby.

Cesarean Rate Rises to Highest Ever Reported in the United States – 32%

ALARMING CESAREAN RATES! [59]

If a mother is on her back, she will have a lot of labor discomfort. She might desire a normal, vaginal birth, and so she tries. She tries so hard. But, in the end, she is forced to believe that she cannot give birth the normal way. We feel so much for these mothers. They do not know how the whole team works against them rather than for them. Unfortunately, fear makes is too easy to use intervention when it is not needed. Please remember that when necessary, anesthesia is okay to use by a skilled professional. There is no need to have guilty feelings. But, be sure that when you decide to use it, that you use it only when necessary.

What positions should the mother be in during birth?

The key is to use what best suits you. The hospital is not happy with you wandering around (though the maternity wards are getting more mother-friendly). There are many ways to give birth: laying on your side, sitting, semi-sitting, birth stool, squatting, semi-squat, hands and knees, and standing. Let's take a look at Moses' birth:

> Then the king of Egypt spoke to the Hebrew midwives, one of whom was named Shiphrah, and the other was named Puah; and he said, "When you are helping the Hebrew women to give birth and see them upon the birthstool, if it is a son, then you shall put him to death; but if it is a daughter, then she shall live." But the midwives feared God, and did not do as the king of Egypt had commanded them, but let the boys live. So the king of Egypt called for the midwives, and said to them, "Why have you done this thing, and let the boys live?" And the

---

[59] Cesarean 2007 statistics: http://www.cdc.gov/nchs/data/databriefs/db35.pdf

midwives said to Pharaoh, "Because the Hebrew women are not as the Egyptian women; for they are vigorous, and they give birth before the midwife can get to them." So God was good to the midwives, and the people multiplied, and became very mighty. And it came about because the midwives feared God, that He established households for them (Ex 1:15-21).

We are not trying to say that because the Israelites were born on a birth-stool all mothers should give birth that way. We are simply trying to point out that the methods we use should cooperate with God's scientific laws, like gravity. The mother squatting or sitting on a birth-stool makes a whole lot of sense. The baby is coming down the canal rather than across, as it is when she is laying down. A birth-stool looks more like a half-moon, which gives something for the Mom to sit on as well as allows the baby to freely come out. Here is a description of another Bible-recorded birth.

Now his daughter-in-law, Phinehas' wife, was pregnant and about to give birth; and when she heard the news that the ark of God was taken and that her father-in-law and her husband had died, she kneeled down and gave birth, for her pains came upon her (1 Sam 4:19).

The problem is that often hospitals greatly limit your options. Don't be afraid to talk to them and work something out.

Should I feel reluctant to talk to the obstetrician?

The parents-to-be should not feel at all reluctant to speak to the obstetrician about their concerns. But probably, to gain the most in the conversation, you will need to do some reading on your own time. We have had eight babies, the second one overseas in a doctor's small, private hospital. We were so glad that we went to a midwife for the delivery of our first baby. At that time, it was primarily because of costs because we did not have money for the hospital. Later on, though, we chose the midwife out of preference.

The doctor, in typical doctor fashion, rushes through the meetings with each patient (expecting mother), and has a quick solution for every problem. They write off this or that prescription. But ignorance is the beginning of fears, especially if the mother has hardly any idea of what to expect. The hospitals have their own expectations. Doctors only have so much time per patient. Many of the hospitals have resorted to birth classes for the parents. Again, if you are well-read, then you can foresee possible problems and talk to your doctor to see if he or she is open to your preferred options.

Are episiotomies necessary?

Episiotomies (a cut is made in the perineum) in most hospitals were regularly given for vaginal births. This cut was made because it was believed that the baby could come out more easily. It is said that an episiotomy is easier to stitch than a natural tear, but the fact is that a tear is not usually nearly as big as a surgical incision, and it can easily be stitched, in addition to healing with less discomfort for the new mom.

Episiotomy and tears can mostly be avoided by a good birth position—squatting, side-lying etc. It is also important to support the perineum as the baby comes out. It is a good comfort measure to have very warm cloths ready to hold on the perineum at crowning. It is important not to push vigorously at the point of crowning.

Why are so many women getting cesarean sections (c-sections)?

One of our greatest concerns is the high rate of caesareans given to women in the United States. The rate is still increasing to where now more than one out of four births are C-sections.[60] This is totally unnecessary. Sometimes a cesarean operation is necessary, but doctors may think this because their perspective of birth mechanics are bad. The

Cesareans are more dangerous!

doctors are used to seeing people on beds lying down. It is convenient for them. They don't have to bend over. They can look professional.

> Breech positioning involves higher risks for the mother and child, regardless of whether the delivery is vaginal or cesarean. Cesareans are being selected more often in these cases to try to improve the outcome in the face of the increased risks. But the consensus group found scientific data in this area generally inadequate to make firm conclusions about desirability of one approach over the other.

> Most clinical reviews suggest that the cesarean may involve less risk for the premature breech infant, but this may not be true for term breech babies. Several studies indicate vaginal delivery of the uncomplicated term breech infant is preferable because an elective cesarean birth involves risk significant complications for the mother and little or no decrease in the risk of infant death.[61]

---

[60] This particular report can be found at www.cfmidwifery.org . A study by Boston University Study on 4 million births between 1991 and 2001 shows the same conclusion. Caesareans have increased 67 percent to first time "no risk" mothers over 34. While it increased 58 percent for those under 30(UPI 11/19/04). Something is very wrong.

[61] See http://www.the-health-pages.com/women/pregnancy/cesarean.html .

America holds one of the highest rates of caesarean birth. Even the Center of Disease Controls has begun to fight it.[62]

Once a cesarean, always a cesarean?

No, not at all. Since doctors are now using a lateral (side to side cut, lower on the belly), there is less risk of rupturing amy former incisions. Many women each year are trying vaginal births after a cesarean.

Drops for baby eyes at birth

Is silver nitrate safe for a baby's eyes? Silver nitrate burns and is uncomfortable. It can interfere with those first minutes of bonding. Every baby gets the drops now. It is required by the state. Do you know why? The baby can be infected if the mother has active gonorrhea when he is passing through the birth canal. An alternative is an antibiotic ointment for the eyes. If you know that you are infection free, you may waive the procedure.

What is the advantage of using a midwife?

Here are some advantages to seeing a midwife for assistance in birth:

- They spend a lot of time teaching and are very willing to talk about your big and small questions, woman to woman.
- They are interested in the whole family, are empathetic, and have more time to invest in your process.
- Belief in working with the natural process: nutrition, birth, exercise, natural remedies, and support.
- Less intervention for both mother and child.

---

[62] "The rate of cesarean delivery in the United States is among the highest for developed nations (1). Because increased risks for maternal death and morbidity and perinatal morbidity are associated with cesarean delivery, a national health objective for the year 2000 is to reduce the overall rate of cesarean delivery to less than or equal to 15.0 per 100 deliveries...." http://www.cdc.gov/mmwr/preview/mmwrhtml/00036845.htm .

- Family can be together.
- Less machine-oriented (eg. they use hands instead of sonogram).
- Less costly (and are often covered by insurance programs).

Summary

God has wonderfully designed the birth process for both humans and animals. He is the specialist of our bodies. We are in charge of our health and bodies, and we must learn to protect ourselves and our children. On the other hand, we need to be more thankful to such a great God who wonderfully cares for us. He is not only the One who gives life, but he watches over every birth.

Although many lives are spared and children helped because of the available interventions at birth, parents need to be vigilant about the over-medicalization of the birth process. With the birth of the internet, plenty of information is at our fingertips. We wanted to make parents aware of possible issues in this chapter so that they can do more research for themselves and form appropriate questions. The return of the midwives is a good sign of a return to natural childbirth. Maternity wards are much more mother and baby friendly.

#4 Study Questions

1. Are any children accidents? Why or why not?

2. What part does God play in the design of each child? How do you know?

3. David and Bathsheba had a child. What can we learn about David's response to this child's early death?

4. How does the dedication and expression of our trust in God for a child protect the heart of the parent in distressing times?

5. How do we know that a child's birth place does not dictate whether he or she will be a great godly man or woman?

6. Are you or your doctor responsible for the decisions for your health?

7. Is anesthesia necessary? If so, why?

8. Is electronic fetal monitoring needed? What problems can it potentially induce?

9. What are a few good positions for birth? What is a bad one? Which is used at hospitals?

10. Why has the occurrence of C-section birth in America risen so high? How can it be avoided?

Godly Beginnings for the Family ARRIVAL

Tender Care for the Newborn

God has not only created an astonishing birth process, but also a marvelous nurturing process. God's design of a mother's warm embrace, provision, and soft voice not only meet the child's physical needs, but also aid in the very long process of training the heart of the child. God intentionally designed woman with all her features. The first woman, Eve, received her name from her distinct ability to bring life into the world. 'Eve' means 'living.'

"Now the man called his wife's name Eve, because she was the mother of all the living" (Genesis 3:20).

The mother can trust God completely, not only with the possibility of problems during birth, but also with nursing, which is designed to meet the needs of the newborn.

But women shall be preserved through the bearing of children if they continue in faith and love and sanctity with self-restraint"(1 Tim 2:15).[63]

Throughout this chapter, we will pay special attention to the post-birth needs of the Mom and newborn. Some things might seem basic to you, and that's fine. We are particularly concerned with those who missed the opportunity to observe their mother caring for younger siblings. This is happening more and more as family sizes shrink. If the family has only one child, that child is likely to miss the opportunity of watching the mothering process in action, which is one reason there are an increasing number of books on the topic. We encourage you to read two books on caring for infants, including one that specializes on nursing. You want to build up your knowledge. Doctors are too busy to answer the many questions mothers have. When choosing your books, though, do be careful. Many books have a secular and unbiblical perspective.

However, it is also good to have an experienced mother that you can feel free to call anytime. As you approach birth, find a mother that you respect and ask her if she would be available to answer your questions. The important thing is that she is agreeable to receive phone calls at any time, even at night. That brings a lot of confidence to the new Mom.

---

[63] 1 Timothy 2:15 is admittedly a difficult text to understand. The word for 'preserved' here is really 'saved.' The Lord is not saying that a woman is saved through having children but that her salvation is to be worked out through having children and preserved through godly behavior. We can understand this more easily as we see women rejecting their God-given responsibilities in marriage as they did back in the time of this letter. Women need to embrace this special task of bearing and nurturing children. Back then it was because they thought they could be closer to God by refraining from sexual activities, which they deemed evil (cf. 1 Timothy 3:1-6). Today it is often because they seek more comfortable and luxurious lifestyles.

Special Care for the Mom

What should Mom expect in the first weeks after delivering a baby? What should others expect of her?

Let's start with the last question first. It is best that, for the first three weeks or so, the mother is able to focus on the dual tasks of personally recuperating and caring for her infant.

"FROM THE MOUTH OF INFANTS AND NURSING BABES THOU HAST ESTABLISHED STRENGTH, BECAUSE OF THINE ADVERSARIES, TO MAKE THE ENEMY AND THE REVENGEFUL CEASE" (PSALM 8:2).

The mother needs someone to care for the regular household duties. Many cultures have certain restrictions or guidelines for the Mom and the new baby. The Chinese mother, for example, is to observe a month of extended rest and care. No matter what society you live in, it is good to have someone to help with meals, household duties, and the other children.[64]

When Linda and I were still having children, her mother came to help out for a week or two (depending how early the baby arrived), which was a significant help. This kind of arrangement, however, is happening less and less. Sometimes parents are unable to help much because of their own jobs, or because they live overseas. In these situations, there arises an opportunity for the church family to help express God's great love by bringing over meals and offering a helping hand. Our societies and families are not poised to care for others as they ought to be.

---

[64] To be honest, couples face many problems with their visiting parents. This is due partly to unresolved conflict from the past as well as different opinions on how to care for the newborn. A whole chapter, also by us, in Principles and Practices of Biblical Parenting discusses this in more detail.

God has designed the mother's body to be able to go through intense adjustments during this time. Remember, for example, at the end of pregnancy how the mother's pelvic bones loosen so that the baby can be born. After birth, the bones readjust, which is accompanied by all sorts of aches and pains. We praise God for the way He takes care of this healing process right down to adjusting body chemicals through hormone changes, but in any case, we should not think the Mom is ready to clean the house any time soon!

Because Linda used the midwife, she would come home about 4-6 hours after the baby was born. She needs to pay more attention to some matters. She often goes through a time when she shivers (even when it is warm). We don't get nervous but just realize it is part of the readjustment process. There will be some bleeding, and pads will be needed. The longer Mom is in the hospital for whatever reason, these needs will be met. Since hospital stays are down to about two days, however, mothers need to better understand the special post-birth needs.

Of course, any surgery or stitching will make a new mother tender. Especially nowadays, mothers are concerned about getting rid of post-baby 'pooch', but a new mother should be more concerned about eating well, getting moderate exercise, and resting her body even more. Sometimes the extra weight will hang around a bit longer if the mother is older (skin is less elastic) or if she was not eating properly before birth. The Mom should be eating lots of good nutritious things not only for herself but also for the baby. What the Mom eats will be passed on to the baby through the breast milk.

So although the mother is recuperating, she needs to prepare herself to care for the infant. Even though others will hopefully be helping her in the beginning, the mother should take over these responsibilities as much and as soon as possible. Nursing and caring helps create a close bond between the mother and the child. Some authors certainly have exaggerated this bonding process, but the fact remains: God has made the mother to be close to the baby. Mothers have a special gentleness that fathers aren't especially gifted with.

The mother should expect to need more naps and fewer long periods of sleep. This works out fine if the mother is not under any pressure from outside activities. The baby will need to be fed and changed regularly. God has already been preparing the mother by having her get up during the nights to visit the bathroom

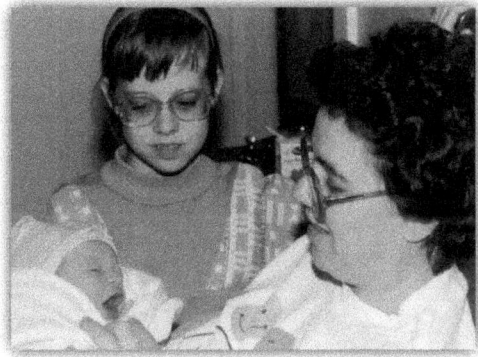

Linda with our oldest daughter, Elizabeth, at the birth of Allison, our third girl.

before birth. She should expect to feed the baby every three hours at first. This schedule will change after 3-4 months, or when the baby starts to stay awake longer and the length of each cycle is extended. More details on establishing a schedule will be given below.

Breastfeeding

We have noted in chapter three the benefits of breastfeeding. Clearly, this is God's way to provide both for the baby's nutritional needs as well as for love and comfort. The mother is called to and designed for this special nurturing time. As much as the mother accepts her calling, she will gain grace, strength, and love to do a great job. Good mothers live by faith in God's grace.

Mothers can feel rather awkward when they first try to breastfeed. It is one thing to read books or watch a video of another mother doing it, but it's another thing when trying it yourself. The process is quite straightforward, but there are a few tricks that can help a mother out so that she does not give up.

The availability of formula makes giving up an easier option when you encounter a few difficulties. It is so much better to breastfeed. The mother's nipples can get sore at first, especially if the baby is not properly latching on. Linda had to relearn the process each time she had a baby. A midwife or nurse will give some pointers. You should not feel awkward asking questions. Although the milk is there after a few days, sometimes it is not so easy to get the milk into the baby!

Sore nipples can be helped by:

- Using vitamin E oil or a lanolin based product to keep them supple.
- Making sure the baby is latched on correctly.

Sometimes formula is necessary. The doctor or nurse should be able to see if the breast is not working properly, but this is rare. The baby can get used to the bottle's easy access to milk, which makes it difficult for the baby to learn how to suck from the breast. The sucking process is quite different. This is the reason it is good to refrain from bottle-feeding early on. Start to nurse the baby right after delivery.

You might be concerned about the nutrition of the baby before the milk comes in. The baby has enough body fat for this transition time. The baby will loose a little weight (up to a pound) after birth before the milk comes in, but remember that this is normal. God provides colostrum, the first substance in the breast, to beef up the baby's immune system. Meanwhile, use this time to train the baby to suck, train the mom to feed properly, and keep Mom and the baby close together. Water is not usually needed.

M O T H E R I N G

There are many other questions that come up. Fortunately, there are many good books with lots of detail on breastfeeding. Some of the breastfeeding questions that you should pay attention to include:

- What does it mean for the baby to be properly latched?
- Does the position of the baby during breastfeeding make a difference? How?
- What should a mother expect when the milk comes in?
- What if the mother can't breastfeed for a day or two? Is it possible to get back on track?
- How do you deal with engorgement and leaking?

We want to acknowledge that many mothers have such concerns. Learn about them ahead of time so you won't be so tempted to give up when you face some difficulty. Don't think that you are the only one facing such problems; refuse to believe that you are a failure. Breastfeeding is simply a new skill to learn.

The Mother, the Nurturer

The mother is God's appointed nurturer for the child. He has not only provided her the physical features for this, but also the psychological design. God has prepared the mother to be able to endure this intensive time of infant care. The mother needs to talk to God, often for endurance, but also for tenderness to rightly care for the newborn with a proper attitude. Notice the way the mother is described below.

> But we proved to be gently among you, as a nursing mother tenderly cares for her own children. Having thus a fond affection for you, we were well-pleased to impart to you not only the gospel of God but also our own lives, because you had become very dear to us (1 Thes 2:7-8).

This is not the time for the mother to think that her husband should spend equal time caring for the baby. God did not give him the features, physically or emotionally, to do this. When a couple believes both husband and wife should share equal time caring for the baby, friction increases between them. They both end up physically and emotionally wiped out. Instead of helping each other, they are bitter and angry toward each other.

Let us be more specific. It's true: the mother could pump so that the father could do the one a.m. feeding, but this is clearly not God's intention. If the mother doesn't breastfeed, then the expectation for the father to help can increase even more, causing yet more friction. It should not. The mother should generally be the primary nurturer except in emergencies.

I find it interesting that the angel of the Lord appeared twice to Samson's mother rather than to his father. Why? It seems rather obvious. She, as the prime nurturer, was given special directions on how she was to care for him.

> "Now therefore, be careful not to drink wine or strong drink, nor eat any unclean thing" (Jud 13:4).

Even more interesting is that when Samson's father found out and asked about special directions, the angel merely told him, "Let the woman pay attention to all that I said" (Judges 13:13). In normal circumstances the wife will care for such duties. The more clearly the husband and wife can define their responsibilities and accept them, the less stress there will be on their relationship. For example, the husband and wife won't let the baby cry for five minutes hoping that the other spouse will care for his needs. Instead, the mother should respond to the baby's needs as if she were serving the Lord Jesus. She is, after all, caring for God's new creation.

The Father: Provider and Overseer

What about the father? Doesn't he have any responsibility toward his wife and newborn? Yes, but his primary role is one of defender, provider, and overseer. The husband will be able to help here and there, but should be able to sleep through the night as much as possible for his regular work routine. Clearly, his role is not the same as the mother's. He oversees the special needs of the family. Because of this new birth, he should keep a closer eye on the needs of his family. If the father can get off from work, a father's role might be the chief support person for the wife when there is no other help around. In other cases, when grandma is visiting, then the husband can show care for his wife and love his child as occasion provides.

How can the father help? It would be great to take a few days off from work so that he can make sure supplies are fully stocked and other needs are attended to. Maybe his wife needs a back rub (or many of them!), or an errand run. The mother, however, should not get upset that the husband does not regularly share in the hard work of caring for the baby. The father should get involved in care for the baby, but much of this bonding is excessive and results in ongoing role confusion.

The husband should run to help if the baby has a mess that spilled over and the mom needs an extra hand. He should talk to her about special concerns such as the importance of talking with a doctor for some problem. The husband should be praying and taking a special interest in family affairs. If she is burdened down, sick, or needy, he should be ready to provide help. The husband can show special delight in his wife by staying pure in mind and patiently waiting for his wife to fully recuperate so that they can be intimate again.

A number of husbands openly demand or secretly expect that their wives will work both outside the home and care for their children at home. God wants the wife home caring for the children. It is better that the couple live in a poorer neighborhood with a used car than for the wife to be working outside the home so that they can afford a nicer home and two cars. The scriptures clearly appoint her to care for domestic and child responsibilities. Professional women who become mothers often face a difficult transition when they return to work. This again is primarily due to the expectations of others and herself that she should work. It will take time to be fulfilled as a mother.[65]

The father is responsible for setting up a Godly home. Decisions need to be made that conform to God's standards. We can't have both God and the world. Wives at home face a lot of pressure and husbands must reinforce the importance of her responsibilities by praising and encouraging her. Although the world encourages the wife to go back to the work force as soon as possible, the need for her to be at home goes way beyond nursing the baby for a few weeks. This will become very evident in the next few chapters on training.

The things that a young child can gain from a mom's constant care is much greater than the supposed 'education' that a child might get at a nursery or preschool. God's design is the best and is fully operable within this modern society.

––––––––––––––––

[65] Parents sometimes only encourage their daughters to succeed in school and fail to encourage them to foster a love for motherhood. No wonder it is so difficult to regain a vision for God's design for them. Paul's caution in 1 Tim 2:14-15 must be remembered. Proverbs 31 will help the mother realize that it is possible to incorporate work, a husband, and a family.

Special Care for the Newborn

There are many incidental items to get in order to properly prepare for a newborn. Below we have a picture of a changing table. A high changing spot is very helpful for changing diapers and clothing. NEVER, NEVER leave the baby alone on the changing table. Here are some items for that changing table or corner:

Diapers: Early on we used cloth diapers but found that disposables are much better and cleaner. However, some parents are rightly concerned with a cleaner environment. Linda has eczema on her hands so rinsing and washing cloth diapers aggravated this condition. When the time it took to wash, purchase, and clean was taken into consideration, the price wasn't that much different. But cloth diapers are making a comeback with many choices for cute covers and even diaper service that makes using cloth diapers more convenient. As new parents, you must think about what is best for your time and money, and thus choose appropriately.

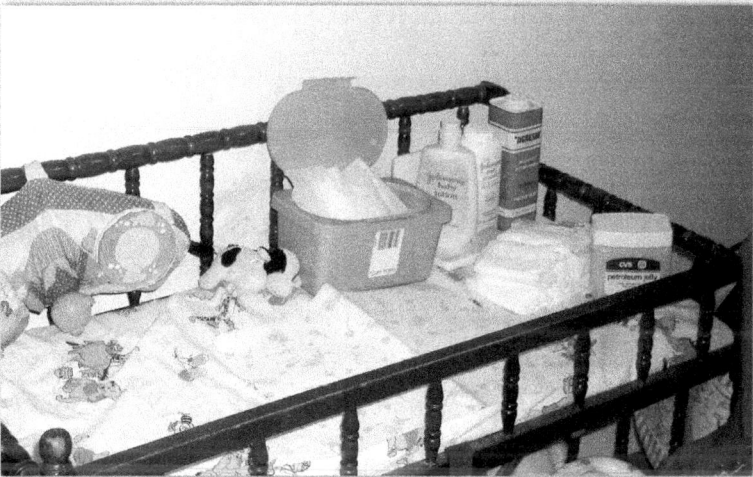

A STOCKED CHANGING TABLE

Vaseline: Petroleum jelly is cheap and a great help. It provides a barrier on broken skin that promotes the healing of diaper rashes and other skin ailments. Linda personally preferred A&D ointment for diaper rash because of the vitamins that promote healing. Balmex is also good because it contains zinc oxide, which is also good for healing skin. But these ointments cannot be used with cloth diapers. Be sure to do some research before you decide on which ointment to use.

Wipes: They are great for a good cleaning. Unfortunately, the child or the mother's hands might be allergic. Damp tissues can be prepared ahead of time. Cotton squares dampened with water also serve the purpose.

Toys: Toys for children so young are merely for show. Infants don't care. When the child is older though, it is very good to have something that keeps their hands occupied.

Powder: While not necessary with the new absorbent disposable diapers, this can help to provide a little extra healing when there is extra dampness or rash. Prickly heat, or lots of little red spots, can bother babies. Cornstarch is also helpful for this purpose.

Other things: Mom should have on hand a thermometer, nose cleaner, ear swabs, and cotton balls.

When the baby is born, the belly button area will need to be cleaned with rubbing alcohol until the cord falls off and is fully healed. God takes care of everything so long as you keep it clean and dry. Remember to be careful when carrying the baby around. We do not recommend having hot items like coffee near the baby because, regardless of how careful you might be, accidents do happen.

Other Matters

Siblings: It is good for your other children to watch and participate as much as possible. They will likely be best friends in the future. If the older sibling(s) feel(s) left out rather than blessed by the newborn, they may revert to some baby-like ways of acting as a means of getting your attention.

Parental attitudes toward the new baby/sibling relationship is vital to harmony between them. Little children love to help out; it will take more time for them to help you with a task, but it is good character training.

Children are good go-getters. Do you need the diaper bag? Have him bring it to you. Let the little one touch the new baby. As they do, emphasize how they are the big brother or sister now. God has made them to help care for the little one. Start this training early on. This is God's birth order. There is responsibility built into the relative ages of the children. We would be wise to work with God's system.

Bathing: Linda used the kitchen sink to bathe our infants. Once it is properly cleaned, the sink is high, handy and has a convenient shelf next to it where she can lay the towel and other necessary items. Again, never leave the baby alone.

Burping: Some babies gulp down their milk, which, without proper burping, can cause air to build up in their stomach and prompt milk 'run over.' This happens more easily with bottle feeding. When breastfeeding, burp the child once or twice during feeding from each side. Do it more if the baby starts to squirm or seems uncomfortable. For the first months, we have a burp diaper to use on the shoulder or under the baby's chin to minimize the mess from the baby's spit-up. Not all babies spit up. If your baby spits up at every feeding, you may need to check your diet for something that disagrees with him. If he spits up very forcefully (projectile vomiting) after most feedings and is losing weight call your doctor. He may have an obstruction.

Know if you need help: The new Mom should not feel left alone, feeling as though there is no one to contact. Nor should she should feel like she is being a bother. At the beginning of this chapter we suggested that you not just have your doctor's telephone number, but have other mom's and support persons' phone numbers that you can call. Do learn what you should look for so that you call your doctor only when there are real problems. We suggest that if the baby is not gaining weight or has a very high temperature, that the doctor be called. An experienced Mom should be able to advise in most other situations. Remember that the doctor is not the grandmother; a good experienced mother is much more willing to give the new mother time and a listening ear.

Rashes: We need to be aware that certain clothes, heat, and lotions can irritate a baby's skin. We need to quickly isolate what the problem is. How we hate to see a baby suffer!

Immunizations: We recommend that infants not get all the vaccines that the doctors will try to give them at birth. Try to wait a while. Space them apart so the baby's immune system is not overtaxed. Get to know the advantages and dangers of vaccines. Some report that the success of vaccines is not due to the vaccines but to the general increase in hygiene and better nutrition. The statistics are worth looking at. Remember, we ought to allow knowledge, not fear, to guide us in making the best decisions. There is a wealth of information on the web, both for and against these vaccinations. Read up and be aware. Don't be intimidated by your doctor! We have supplied more information in the appendix.

Advantages of Infant Routine

The baby's first day is marked by trauma. Imagine coming out of the dark, warm womb into the bright, cold experience of artificial light and air. The little one, however, will quickly settle into this new situation. Babies don't know what works or what is supposed to happen. They learn by experience. When young, babies are unaware of various aspects of their bodies. They will first begin to master their sounds and mouth.

FEEDING TIME	AWAKE TIME	SLEEPING TIME
There are three parts to the infant's routine: feeding, awake and sleeping. This routine will repeat itself over and over throughout the day. Each cycle will take about 3 hours for a newborn to a 3-4 month old baby. The number of times this routine will repeat will lessen as the baby begins to sleep longer and eventually through the night.		
After the milk comes in and the baby adjusts to nursing, the feeding time will normalize and will not change until later.	At first, the awake period will be minimal or even nonexistent. The baby will tend to sleep quite a bit. But this awake time will stretch as the baby grows.	The baby will adjust to going to sleep by itself and sleeping by itself. The big hope is for the baby to sleep through the night by 8-10 weeks.

BABY FEEDING SCHEDULE

Training the baby starts on day one. The way a mother responds to the baby's noise or movement will greatly shape how the baby will respond in the future. They are learning through every experience. If the baby is pleased with the result of what he does, such as receiving some warm milk, then this will reinforce the baby's willingness to repeat that action.

The parents are often oblivious to the important lessons taking place that are shaping the child's life. They are trying really hard to meet all the baby's needs, but they also need to remember that their devoted attention of love in the first week or two of the baby's life is setting a pattern.

Some parents have a hard time accepting routines. It might seem a bit rigid with a baby who doesn't understand much of anything, and we certainly understand these concerns, but there are two choices. Either we will 1) allow the baby to orchestrate the timing of things through its cries or 2) the parent will orchestrate the timing of things with a thought-out routine. Beneath the surface of these two approaches are differing philosophies. Some parents are taught that the baby knows best. This understanding is rooted in modern philosophy, which states that the animal nature in a person is most happy when fulfilled.[66] This is unbiblical and many modern day problems stem from this. But in order to keep things simple[67] we will focus on God's design. God knows what is best for children because He created them. He has revealed His knowledge in the Bible to the parents and has given them the knowledge and wisdom to know what is best for their children. Modern parenting, however, expects the parents to allow the child to dictate what is best.

For example, if we allow the baby to dictate when he should be fed, then the child will be cry-oriented. Only by crying can the baby let the mother know he is hungry. So the baby cries to get fed. But the baby also notices he gets warmth, a soft voice, and all sorts of good

---

[66] The popularizing of Rousseau's unbiblical philosophy of life has largely shaped modern life styles.

[67] We have written in length of this corruption at www.foundationsforfreedom.net/Topics/Family/Parenting011_SecularDev.html

things when he cries. He will confuse warmth with feeding. The signal will be muddied, and the mother will become subject to the baby's confusion. All babies like to be held close. The time when the baby is held is usually when he is being nursed. When the mother puts the baby down (to get her own rest), she tiptoes out. But once the baby is not feeling that warmth, the baby will cry.

Now the mother *and* the child will get confused as to what the other really needs. If the only way the baby can communicate that he wants to be held is to cry, then he will cry to be held. The baby likes being held. However, the mother can't be sure if the baby is hungry or not because the baby cries a lot just to be held. The longer this happens, the worse the confusion gets. More than this, when the baby is being fed at short intervals (when it cries) partly in order to soothe the baby, his hunger cycle gets confused. He is only getting snacks, not a full feeding.

Sure, the baby is contented with less, but this approach will require that the baby eats more frequently. The mother's breast on the other hand will produce only as much milk as what is being taken. If the feedings are short, then the mother will only produce this much milk. Furthermore, if the mother is nursing the baby very frequently, her breasts can get sore very quickly. But of course, if she takes a break, then the baby cries. The mother might feel guilty, and the husband and in-laws all might get very mad at mother. They do not think she is doing a good job because the baby is crying. We feel for these mothers because they are trying so hard and yet are still feeling rejected. This rejection is usually passed on to the child through the mother's frustrations.

Is it wrong to allow a baby to cry? Many people think so. We respond with two things.

1) If short-term crying encourages the baby to adapt to a routine where crying happens less often, then it is okay.

2) Second, responding to the baby's cries will shape a desire-oriented child. The child will grow up expecting others to conform to his will. This is clearly counter to the principle of love (the sum of all morality) wherein Christians are to be other-oriented.

Perhaps, as a caution, we should mention that parents should always be attentive to our baby's cry. Make sure you check the baby for sharp objects, gas, wet or dirty diapers, or sick with a fever. In our above comments about crying, we are focusing on a child regularly using crying (same way each time) to get something he wants. This can become controlling. Though the mother will feel like she is doing her job, she will become exhausted.

Routine has wonderful short-term and long-term advantages because it follows God's order of things: the parents deciding what is best for the children. Children are foolish and will fall into bad habits if parents are not watchful. Parents need to guide the child; the child does not dictate to the parents.

Short-term benefits include predictability. The mother can get some definite sleep even if it is in the form of a nap of a few hours at first. Because of the routine, the mother knows when the baby will be hungry and can feed the baby. The baby and Mom will feed quicker without all the extra stress from crying. They both anticipate the feeding (eg. mother's let-down reflex). The baby will sleep better. This enables the child (and mother) to be of better temperament. The baby will cry less often, so therefore the mother can distinguish the needs of the baby from his or her cry. The mother will be confident. Everyone else is happy because the baby is happier. The joy of the process will become very evident.

The long-term effects of this process are powerful. We will speak more about this in a later chapter, but a routine will help build security into the child through expectation and reward. Infants are more willing to wait when they have a better understanding of what will be coming. For example, if they know they will be fed soon after waking up, then they do not need to cry to get the milk. This 'waiting power' feeds into the whole process of building moral character in the child. The child will not be desire-oriented. They will instead develop patience and the ability to wait.

The mother and child should get into a routine as soon as possible. I will outline a baby routine that worked very well for Linda and myself in a later chapter.[68]

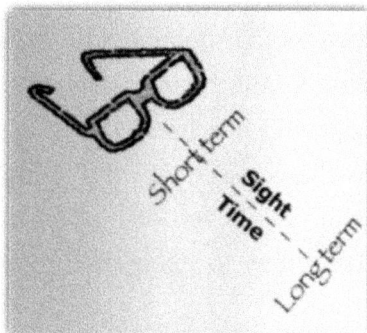

If you anticipate disruptions to the routine, like on a busy Sunday or while traveling, just work back into it. If the baby is very sleepy, try different things to keep him awake: partly undress him, wipe his bare feet with cold water, wipe his face with cool water. You want him to take a full feeding. If nothing else works, let him sleep, but do not feed him again until the next feeding in your routine. This is very hard for the mother to do if he wakes early and you know he is hungry. Try to wait.

Routine should be kept somewhat flexible. Rigidly keeping to the routine can cause you to ignore some real needs. The mother should understand the child's needs, and the child will learn how to be blessed by another who comes and cares for him. Respond to him in a timely but unhurried manner. God's ways are the best.

This early routine is important. We are encouraging you to work toward a good routine. It won't happen overnight, but the earlier you start, the better it will be for everyone. The next chapters will

---

[68] We are grateful for Gary Ezzo's explanation of this particular schedule. Blended with lots of love, it works!

address training, in which we will not only instruct you about how things are done but also why.

Summary

The first two months following birth will pass all too quickly. Don't get so involved in the process that you forget to enjoy the beautiful moments with your gift from God. Reading books and listening to Mozart might help, but we need to remember that Jesus grew up just fine without modern gimmicks. Of more importance is the consistent and patient care that the mother provides for the child. We are not just caring for the child's bodily needs but are beginning to shape their inner lives.

#5 Study Questions

1. How does a mother's tender nursing care for the child's needs?

2. Childbirth is a holy role for women. <u>1 Timothy 2:15</u> says that their souls will be _____ or saved through the bearing of children if they continue in faith, love and sanctity.

3. What kind of help does a mother with a newborn need?

4. How did God's design of pregnancy physically prepare the mother before birth for the special care she would need to give to her child after birth?

5. Why shouldn't a wife expect the husband to split the time caring for their newborn? Any Biblical basis for this?

6. How does a mother know she can handle everything?

7. Does a mother remember how to properly feed the baby with subsequent births? Why?

8. A mother of a newborn has lots of questions. When should she call the doctor? Who else could she make arrangements with ahead of time to be able to call?

9. What is the problem with infant immunizations?

10. What are the two methods of raising the child? How is this choice confirmed by the way a mother responds to the baby's needs?

11. What are some special responsibilities for the father after the birth of the child?

12. How should a couple work through the various expectations for the wife to work after having a child.

13. List four short-term advantages to having an infant routine.

14. What is one long-term advantage of having an infant routine?

15. What does the routine of a baby look like? Is the order important? Why or why not?

$\mathcal{G}$odly Beginnings for the Family ARRIVAL

The Challenge of Child Training

Something intrigues me about Daniel, the young Hebrew man who was taken as a captive to a distant country. He and several of his noble friends were chosen to compete with others through special training for service to the king of Babylon.

By choosing to eat differently than the others, Daniel chose to risk his opportunity to be selected to be included in the king's chosen elite. He chose to obey God. What made him take such a risk?

The rest of the Book of Daniel clearly proves that he was not stupid, nor was he a spiritual 'loner.' He became a wise and mighty ruler. We cannot go into the whole story here, but it brings before us a question that we should reflect on as parents-to-be or parents with young children. What motivated Daniel? What made this young man so different from the rest? What choices did he make that distinguished him? We started a list to answer these questions:

• Daniel refused to stoop to self-pity over the loss of his parents, country, manhood, and everything familiar. Instead, he embraced the present situation as from God. He refused to be bitter over his losses and chose instead for God to be his most loyal and trustworthy friend.

- Daniel refused to compromise his faith for the easy assimilation into the dominating pagan culture.

- Daniel discerned the importance of spiritual purity in a very impure spiritual environment.

- Daniel exercised self-control by resisting the temptation to enjoy the regular royal meals and instead choosing vegetarian meals. (Remember that young men can really eat!)

- Daniel chose to risk the emperor's special selection in order to remain pure before God. God's pleasure was his priority.

- Daniel resisted intimidation by foreign supervisors in order to do what he sensed was right (persisted with the overseer).

- Daniel stood alone in the fear of God. Even his three friends seemed to follow Daniel rather than lead him, though they were in support of him.

When we look deeper into his decision not to eat the king's food, we note that there were many values that shaped Daniel's decision. It is the subtle but powerful, uncompromising purpose of Daniel that God used to make an impact on the lives of the readers of Daniel 1.

What shaped Daniel? What enabled him to resist the temptation to compromise and potentially lose a luxurious and famous career at a time when he had absolutely nothing, just so he could remain faithful to God?

We might contrast Daniel's situations to one of the greatest fears of parents: "What will my children do when they are away from me?"

Hundreds of thousands of these fears prove themselves to be founded in reason each year when children leave home for college or their own apartments and commit themselves to this adulterous world. Daniel's life shows us that it is possible to raise a different kind of young man or woman. But we must ask another question: "How can we raise such young men and women of faith in this adulterous generation?"

Sometimes when we ask what we want our children to be, we are usually thinking of what profession or line of work we would hope for them to succeed in. But what good is it if our children gain the whole world and lose their soul (Luke 9:25)? Outstanding characters like Joseph, Daniel, and Jesus, among many others, remind us that our profession is a side point when it comes to the question of our character. Godly training is everything because it serves as a foundation. Once the godly training has begun (though it has not been completed), we can only then think of activities and profession: a godly businessman, a godly repairman, a godly pastor, or a godly homemaker. We will end up compromising if we do not have a foundation.

> "Be on guard, that your hearts may not be weighted down with dissipation and drunkenness and the worries of life, and that day come on you suddenly like a trap; for it will come upon all those who dwell on the face of all the earth. But keep on the alert at all times, praying in order that you may have strength to escape all these things that are about to take place, and to stand before the Son of Man" (Luke 21:34-36).

> For what does it profit a man to gain the whole world, and forfeit his soul? (Mark 8:36)

Such devotion and dedication does not happen by accident. There is no doubt that part of the influence in Daniel's life was parental.

Only godly parents can raise godly children. Since Daniel and his friends were of noble families, tutors probably also trained them. Our question, then, is "How could there be good parents or a good prophet during a time in which Israel had left God?" We find a clue when Isaiah addresses King Hezekiah, the last king before the invasion.

> And some of your sons who shall issue from you, whom you shall beget, shall be taken away, and they shall become officials in the palace of the king of Babylon (Is 39:7).

King Hezekiah brought renewal to the dying nation of Israel. There is no doubt that God used him and his influence to train not only his sons but perhaps a few other noblemen's sons too. He was one of the rare kings who called upon the Lord. Perhaps Daniel and others even had chances to be instructed by Isaiah the prophet. We do not know for sure what happened, but we do know that some significant godly training took place in their young lives. Godly men are not produced in a vacuum. Daniel was either a son of Hezekiah or a son of another nobleman. The emperor of the Babylonian empire, true to God's prophetic Word, made these young men part of his advisory board.[69]

So let us ask, how do we inculcate these godly perspectives and attitudes into the lives of our children? This is our holy duty before God. This is clearly the most compassionate thing we can do for our children, that they might find God's grace. We need to train our children now so that they will be able to withstand this wicked and adulterous age.

Thought: Why would parents desire that their child "believe in Jesus" while young or even be baptized, but then not follow through with godly training? What will happen to a child so raised?

---

[69] The word for official was eunuch. It was understood that Daniel and his friends would lose more than their home country but also their manhood and the opportunity to marry.

What about all those people out there who are living lascivious lives who once confessed to being Christians when young? (cf. 1 Cor 6:9-11; 2 Cor 13:5).

The Need for Training

All parents start off training the same way: a tiny baby, God's special creation, lies in your arms. Your job is to shape him or her into a godly man or woman. But because the baby has inherited the parents' sin nature, he/she has an evil heart that makes the job much more difficult. Part of the problem is that the foolish heart of the infant is hidden at first from the eyes and understanding of the parents.

The first week or two of the little one's life enamor the parents so much that they start dreaming of all these great things for their precious child, as well as for their family. What they don't know is that the child's evil heart will slowly begin to reveal and express itself. As the baby grows, he or she will be much more capable of utilizing sounds, gestures, words, and the body to carry out the wishes of his or her sinful heart. We naïve parents are shocked that the child doesn't nicely comply with our good plans.

The scriptures are so clear about the problem and how to solve it. The heart of the child is bound by foolishness. Only discipline and the rod will shake him from blindly following his heart (but please keep in mind that the rod should not be used until the child is able to understand how it is connected to his disobedience to the spoken rule).

> Foolishness is bound up in the heart of a child; the rod of discipline will remove it far from him. (Pr 22:15)

Gifts of beauty, intellect, and personality can make training more difficult for parents. The intellectual are craftier. They have many cute ways to manipulate. The handsome have great struggles with pride. The wealthy have a thousand more ways to get into serious sin than do their poorer cousins. But all children suffer equally the same condition of an evil heart. Godly training does not cure an evil heart, but it does shape the child so that he will be more comfortable with God and His ways, and as a result, he or she will more likely seek out God for himself. As he grows, the child will become increasingly aware of his or her sinful ways and thus will know the need of a Savior.[70] We can see why God exhorts the fathers to be involved in their children's lives, because if they don't, the children will suffer greatly.

> And, fathers, do not provoke your children to anger; but bring
> them up in the discipline and instruction of the Lord (Eph 6:4).

What we do as parents will shape our children's lives. If we leave them to themselves, they will live as the world, controlled by their sinful hearts and desires. However, if we train them in God's way, their lives will have a Godly influence, and they will walk in His way.

> Train up a child in the way
> he should go, Even when he is old he will not depart from it (Pr
> 22:6).

---

[70] We must clearly recognize that even children brought up under godly parents are sinners. Godly training should help a child identify his own sin and thus ready him for knowing the Lord. Godly training does not make the child think he is righteous apart from Christ! This is foolish worldly religion that condemns the child to self-righteousness and its judgment.

Going back to Daniel for a moment, then, how can we get involved in training that produces results like Daniel and his three friends? We have discussed the main things that children need to learn in order to gain moral resolve like Daniel's. We desire that God would fully bless each of our children with gifts, abilities, and resources that he or she can utilize in life. This can only come about if they have godly character.

God decides what gifts He gives to each child. We cannot change that. We are, however, our children's trainers, so we are responsible to lead them well. If we succeed, it is easier for them to find God on their own and live in a way that pleases Him. If we fail, however, we make it very difficult for them. In summary, we want our children to grow like Jesus.

> And Jesus kept increasing in wisdom and stature (age), and in favor with God and men (Luke 2:52).

These words remind us of what is really important. But you might protest, "Jesus was different." You are quite right. Jesus didn't have the evil heart that our children are born with. Without that evil heart, we can see how there would be a good 'natural' growth. We need to be aware that our child, as cute as he is, is wired to do only evil, to live by his own sinful nature. 'Natural' things usually only mean an expression of his wayward heart. So how do we train our children, who have evil hearts?

Thought: Do you really believe your child needs training? Why? What will happen if you neglect to train your child in one or two areas of his or her life?

Understanding the Training of Your Young Children

The things that a baby can learn should surprise us. Babies may be small, but that doesn't hold them back from learning at great rates. Training has to do with shaping what they are learning. We want them to learn the right things from their early experiences. As parents we desire that they learn how to overcome their foolish tendencies and live through right decisions even before they know those decisions are right. Aside from plain ignorance to our responsibilities as parents to train our children, we face two popular assumptions that oppose child training.

Assumption #1: Training is Unnecessary

Some parents will protest and think that it is unnecessary to train children so young. These parents object on the basis that a child is predisposed to being one way or the other. For example, one child is 'naturally' fussy but another is quiet. Another example we often hear is that boys are more 'active.' We agree on the whole that this is true, but that only means they need more consistent training! These parents believe that babies will be babies.[71] And, generally speaking, they reject the necessity of training.[72] They come to the conclusion that they cannot really condition or train their child, nor do they need to.

Of course, when it comes down to it, no parent can be completely consistent with this philosophy. Once in a while, they must say

---

[71] Unfortunately, too many parents have used this excuse to pardon the sinful behavior of their child.

[72] These parents should examine their own upbringing. In many cases their own parents were too strict and they are reacting in an extreme way to this. Please refer to www.foundationsforfreedom.net/Topics/Parenting/Parenting03_Authority.html .

'Stop' or 'Don't do that' in order to restrain the naughty child. But we view this perspective in another way.

If the child's nature is so dominant that change cannot be brought about, then why does the Bible speak so clearly about training and instruction? We choose instead to follow the Bible's teaching and commit ourselves to training the child.

We are not saying that each child does not have his or her own personality, bent, or temperament. Babies tend to have their own natural dispositions and pool of gifts that consist of strengths and weaknesses. From our own experiences, it seems that each child has at least one area of strength and one area of moral weakness. Examples of strengths include being sensitive to the needs of others, helpful, orderly, clean, attentive, knowledgeable, insightful, devoted, etc. Examples of weaknesses are fear, doubt, rash action, worry, explosive anger, sensual tendencies, laziness, deceitful, etc.

> **Personal Names**
>
> Names tend to shape the person. We see this very clearly in scripture where names in both Hebrew and Greek have meanings. As the children grow, we can share with them the kind of person we envision them to be. This helps them more smoothly fit into the good aspect of their name. Let me give you an example.
>
> My name, Paul, means 'little.' It helps me to remember that God delights in using little things in great ways to bring greater glory to His Name.

The Strong-Willed Child

A good friend once mentioned his concern for bringing his baby into this lascivious world. Later, he revealed what he was truly thinking when he said, "What if he is a strong-willed child?" The notion behind his comment is the fear that there is a certain kind of child that cannot be trained. But we need to think about this idea a bit and realize its deceitfulness.

The greatest problem is that people do not think through what a strong-willed child is. It certainly is not a biblical term. Actually, we even see that Daniel showed himself to possess a strong will. Those who are very self-controlled are able to exert an extreme amount of control over their willpower so they can set themselves to do the things that they know please God. This certainly was not my friend's concern. His concern was over a child who was strong-willed in doing evil.

But again, we need to go back and think about what we are really trying to say. First, let's admit that it is not the strong will that is the problem. We should be thankful for strong wills. Second, let us call out the real problem: all children do evil, and some are spoiled rotten. But the problem is not their strong wills but their willingness and ability to do evil, along with the parents' willingness to let it happen. Is there a cure? There sure is!

The scriptures state very clearly that the rod of discipline chases the folly far from a child. The problem is not children who are strong-willed, but parents who will not consistently use chastisement to keep their children from expressing their evil. The more freedom the child has to do evil, the more they go wild, assuming they have the right to get everything they desire. This problem develops, then, not because of a child's temperament but because of the parents' unwillingness to love the child and care for him by proper discipline and training.

As my wife well summarizes, "The problem is not a strong-willed child but a weak-willed parent."

Assumption #2: Unable to Train a Baby

Other parents will reject the idea that children can learn things at such an infant level. True, a baby's thinking process is not the same as a school-aged child. The learning process is more like conditioning them to respond in ways agreeable with what they want.

We can answer these parents in two ways:

God tells us to instruct our children. We should obey Him, even if we do not understand the process.

We recognize the difference between a trained and an untrained one-, three-, and six-month old. The difference is like day and night. Why wait to start training a one-year-old when starting earlier makes it easier for both parent and child?[73] Starting later makes retraining necessary but hard, and even worse, it is rarely done well.

The Means of Training

A child chiefly learns in two ways: imitation and observation. Imitation is obvious. I brought my little two-year-old daughter to say "Hi" to Mom. I saw my little girl make a funny face raising her eyebrows and I wondered what she was doing, when I realized that she was imitating my wife whose face I couldn't see from my position. Children love to imitate sounds, gestures and everything they can. Many parents, however, miss the way that children learn by imitation.

---

[73] Although many of our insights are gathered from observation of both adults and children, our main assumption is that God's design is best. Sinful ways are always worst. We attach unpleasant feelings with expressions of the sin nature and do not reward it. On the other hand we highly reward good responses. For example, when the mother comes in and sees the baby awake waiting to be fed, she says all sorts of nice things in pleasant tones and feeds the baby. Routines allow for this.

Training up godly children

Tiny children also learn quickly from their experiences. They observe what happens in response to what they do. For example, a baby learns that when it cries, a big person will come to see what is wrong, pick him up, and say a lot of nice sounding words. The child, through repeating the process, learns how to connect and communicate to the big world, bit by bit.

The child needs to learn some very basic lessons to be able to grow in wisdom. Training has two aspects to it: rebuke and discipline, both of which curtails their willingness to respond according to the foolishness bound up in their hearts. Training also includes positive exhortation, instruction, and encouragement so that they can grow in wisdom. What are some of these positive areas of training? Let me draw out five specific areas that need to be developed in young children, and some suggestions for how to help them grow in these areas.

Foundational Areas of Training

Five of the most foundational things an infant needs to learn are: security, self-control, trust, contentment, and respect for parents (obedience). These elementary concepts are closely connected to one another and will allow the infant to grow properly and learn to love God and others. Please remember we are not speaking about the way an adult learns. An adult learns by taking in concepts, images, words, ideas, and processes them into useful information by which they make decisions. As stated above, children including infants, learn chiefly by imitation and observation of cause and effect, and they are rewarded with cuddles, soft voices, and gentle care.

You might wonder how security, self-control, and the other character qualities have anything to do with what a baby learns from being picked up. A baby is learning what to expect in life from the situations that he faces. Let's take a brief look at each of these important things a child needs to learn to become a godly child.

1) Security

Security is a sense of tranquility about life that enables a child to respond without fear or anxiety to changing situations. As the child observes what happens in different situations, he finds that he is okay if he hears either of his parent's voices. His trust is a big key in understanding how strong his sense of security is. Security is also closely related to how contented a child is.

Security is learned by normal routines and fulfilled expectations about his key concerns, namely, wet diapers, hunger, or hurt. When something is wrong, he knows from experience that someone will care for him in a timely and pleasant manner. The manner and attitude of the parent's response: patient or impatient, fearful or trusting, anxious or calm, will greatly shape the child's attitude.

The positive attitudes of the parents will generally produce a secure child; negative attitudes and responses from the parents will generally produce an insecure child. Insecurity develops when the child finds that the help he needs is irregular or, when he is older, it comes from sensing the possible loss of those that care for him (eg. toddler observes parents quarreling). Therefore, insecurity in the child is related to the fearful, anxious impatient attitudes of the parent.

2) Self-control

Self-control is the ability to restrain one's own actions, words, or desires in order to do what is right. Because the infant has no self-control, the parent acts on his behalf to cause him to bring his will and desires under the benevolent rule of the parent. In this process, the baby becomes acquainted with what it means to restrain his actions or will in order to conform to the parents' will.

Self-control is gained by knowing the rules or laws, choosing to put one's own will aside and conforming to the rules. As a child gets older, he will internalize these decisions. He will obey even when others are not watching.

This is taught in several ways, but the clearest method at the infant level is simply making sure the child does not get everything he wants when he desires it. This includes not feeding the child when you know he has had sufficient milk, not holding the baby whenever he is awake and not going to get the crying baby when you know he is okay and should be sleeping.

At the infant level, self-control is cultivated by having a good routine. It is enforced by discipline in older children. The lack of self-control is quite apparent when the child is oblivious to the rules around him, and merely seeks to satisfy his interests or desires.

We might think self-control would develop only in older children but we can see the contrasts very clearly in trained and untrained babies. Those 'reachers' or 'crawlers' who are gaining self-control will tend to move more slowly into new situations. They are trying to discern the boundaries from what they already know. "I can't touch that. I can do this." They are comfortable with clear boundaries. Those without self-control are bent on doing their own thing. They rush into situations, assuming they can touch anything. Later, as they begin to crawl or walk, they assume they can go anywhere. They will protest loudly when their will is restrained. Self-control is strongly coupled with obedience.

3) Trust

Trust is the ability to believe certain things can and should happen. Trust, belief, and faith have the same Greek root word, but have different shades of meaning. A child learns trust through observing what normally happens. They know what can happen by observing what does happen. They try things because they see it being done (imitation). If they don't see it done, then they don't try it. Good routines help build up this trust level. Notice how David says that he learned trust.

> *"Yet thou art He who didst bring me*
> *forth from the womb;*
> *Though didst make me trust when upon*
> *my mother's breasts" (Ps 22:9).*

A child's faith and expectation are closely entwined and have a powerful shaping influence on the child's attitude. If the baby in a routine finds that his mother comes for him time after time after he wakes, then he will quickly develop a trust that he will be fed at the right time. He knows someone is caring for him. He does not need to fear or cry. Instead he can in a satisfied way look at the things around him. A baby with little or no routine will tend to cry more because he doesn't know what to expect.

Trust is the ability of the child to endure little modifications in his lifestyle and still not be ruffled. The opposite of trust is fear. Fear also has a strong shaping influence, but it opposite to what is needed at that stage. Love and trust is the first stage of learning. If the mother responds with anxiety, impatience, or worry, the child will also learn to respond to life the same way. Fear is the absence of trust and provokes certain unpleasant responses like panicky cries.

4) Contentment

Contentment is a willingness to be satisfied with the present circumstances. A contented child is a true blessing. And even though some children seem to be more "naturally inclined" to contentment, it is a lesson all children need to learn. A child learns contentment through recognition and acceptance of boundaries: that he cannot have something (an out-of-reach toy) or be somewhere else (cries to get out of the playpen), or do something else (stay at the park a little longer).

Parents sometimes think it is good to give the child many, many toys to stimulate their curiosity. In a matter of minutes, however, the one toy will lose its appeal. The child never really gains an appreciation for the toys because there is always another one to move on to. In fact, contentment allows the child to develop focus and concentration skills.

Too many toys or choices interfere with gaining these skills. Contentment with only a few toys or objects allows a child to gain mastery over fine motor skills. It provides time to explore the intricacies of the textures, colors, sounds, and use of them. Discontentment exposes itself through rudeness and fussiness. Discontented children are not grateful and are poor stewards of what they have because they have not learned to value their possessions.

5) Respect for Authority (Obedience)

Respect for authority is a sense of caution or proper fear toward the ones in authority over them. Healthy fear motivates them to conform to the authority's desires. Obedience is quick compliance to another's commands. A child first learns respect and then obedience. With respect, obedience comes fairly easily.[74] A child will not regularly obey a person they do not respect. They will tend to please themselves.

A baby of course does not understand authority. He is acquainted with only a select number of people who most often care for his

---

[74] Keep in mind that when we mention respect or obedience, we mean a state in which a child tends to act a certain way. They still have a sinful heart and will at times provide exceptions to what they might commonly do.

needs. He learns to respond to them. The baby will gain respect when he is prevented by the caregiver from carrying out his own selfish will. Healthy fear comes later when he is given a little tap with a rod to reinforce the idea that some action is unacceptable.

Repetition of the activity, linked to a tap or a "no" from the parent will cause an unpleasant feeling. In order to avoid the unpleasant feeling and the sense of a frustrated will, he will typically refrain from doing it again. Some babies are more stubborn and will take a longer time to learn. Parental consistency goes a long way to bringing about compliance more quickly. If he learns that "no" always means "no" he will comply more quickly. By sometimes giving into the child's whims, the angst between parent and child increases.

The more respect that exists, the more obedience there will be. It is true that obedience is not our end goal. We do not want them merely obeying us, but that they desire to do what is right and good from their hearts. For this they need the Lord. A lack of respect is cultivated by giving the child freedom to do what he wants. He does not understand authority because authority has not shown itself to be in existence.

6) Other character traits

We do not have time to trace how all the different character traits are learned. We simply want you to recognize that the child who trusts will be more patient than the one who fears. The contented child is more apt to be joyful than the upset and discontented child. The secure child will be more at peace than the insecure child. The self-controlled child will tend to be well-behaved, while the child that lacks self-control will tend to be naughty. The child who respects his parents will do much more goodness.

We can train a child to respond in a loving way by helping him to think about the needs of others and doing something about it only when the child is not preoccupied with getting what he desires. In other words, the ability to exercise control over his own desires enables him to learn how to care for the needs of others.

Once a child has learned to accept limits to his will and desires, then he can learn how to be comfortable with doing what is right, good, and pleasing. Otherwise he will never reach that point. We are not saying that this can replace the Spirit of God in a person, but instead that it readies a child to identify what is the highest good, namely, the love of God as seen in Christ Jesus. He is still a sinner and needs the forgiveness of God in Christ.

Summary

We have observed how a child needs to learn certain basic moral qualities very early in life. If a very young child is acquainted with such pleasing patterns, it will pave the way for them into young adulthood when they will begin to consciously choose what they want in life.

As an example, a woman was once sitting next to our two-year-old, who was was sitting in a folding chair, holding her food and cup in her hands patiently waiting for Mom to return. The lady said to me, "She is just like an adult." We know other families who train their children. They do the same things.

Training brings about mature responses early in a child's life. We don't often see the results of early training because people do not believe it can happen and therefore don't persist in training their young children. If parents focus on keeping a child from doing certain things, they miss the point of discipline. Discipline is the development of an ability and desire to do good.

Daniel is a great reminder for us. He first reminds us that there is a pagan culture out there that wants to swallow up our children. But more importantly, he reminds us that we can greatly shape the character of our children. We can train up our child in the way he should go, and when he is old, he will not depart from it.

#6 Study Questions

1. Name one special characteristic of Daniel that touches you. Why?

2. How do we know there is hope for children born to Christian parents in a pagan age?

3. Was Daniel trained? Explain how Daniel might have received this training.

4. What surprise do we find that comes bundled with every special little new baby? Why so?

5. What does Proverbs 22:15 say about the problem and solution to raising godly children?

6. Does the gifting or natural disposition of a child make it so that any child should not be trained? Explain.

7. Explain the two ways a young child chiefly learns things.

8. Fill in the blank: Training has to do with _____ what they are learning.

9. Why is a 'strong-willed' child not really a problem?

10. How does a child learn trust early on?

11. How does a child learn self-control early on?

12. How does respect for parental authority relate to obedience?

13. A child might be well-trained when young, but he still needs to come to know the Lord. Why?

Godly Beginnings for the Family ROUTINES

The Discipline and Training of Small Children

Once we have caught God's vision for the upbringing of godly children in this immoral world, we need to adjust our training methods. There are two parts to Biblical child training: positive instruction and physical correction. These two work in tandem—if you leave one out, it will no longer be a Biblical method.

(1) Physical correction restrains the expression and development of the child's foolish heart.

(2) Positive instruction trains the child to do the right thing with the right attitude.

Many parents no longer think that they can truly influence their children's lives and behavior, but nothing is further from the truth. All of the proverbs that address the issue of child training confirm the parents' sphere of influence and responsibility to train their children. If the parent fails to train the child by neglect or through improper procedures (such as not utilizing physically correction, or utilizing it incorrectly), the child will suffer the consequences.

157

After describing biblical discipline and its goals, this chapter will give you practical insight on how to train your child from the beginning, up through the toddler stage and beyond.

Understanding Biblical Discipline

The Bible says a lot about the discipline or chastening of children. We can think of the Bible as a training manual on how to raise Godly children. We would like to draw upon numerous biblical principles on child training and discipline from the Book of Proverbs. We have grouped them under five general topics.

The Biblical Way to Discipline	
... But he who loves him disciplines him diligently. (Proverbs 13:24)	For discipline to be effective, it must be consistent.
My son, observe the commandment of your father, And do not forsake the teaching of your mother; (Proverbs 6:20)	A father and mother's instruction is basic to training a child.
Do not hold back discipline from the child, Although you beat him with the rod, he will not die. (Proverbs 23:13)	Although we might not feel like disciplining the child, we must do it for the long-term good of that child.
Do not hold back discipline from the child, Although you beat him with the rod, he will not die. (Proverbs 23:13)	We might fear hurting our child or his emotions with the rod, but we must remember that he will not be damaged by it.

He who gathers in summer is a son who acts wisely, But he who sleeps in harvest is a son who acts shamefully. (Proverbs 10:5)	Training must include areas of responsibility and diligence.

Although the concepts of biblical discipline are clear, our efforts in explaining those concepts in English words are not. Part of the problem is the difference of meaning and associated connotations of some words. Also, part of the difficulty is that some key biblical terms have no good modern English translation.

- The verb 'to discipline' is used to refer to both the physical correction as well as the pursuit of having a 'well-disciplined' or trained child. Unfortunately many people understand the word 'discipline' to mean only spanking, hitting, or beating.

- The word 'chastise'[75] can carry meanings associated with both correction and training; rarely is it used now.

- Instruction refers to the methods that parents use to help a child acquire good habits, skills, self-control, and obedience.

Instead of creating another word, we will use the word 'training' to include aspects of both the physical correction and instruction. When we use the verb 'to discipline,' it will more often than not refer to the aspect of physical correction. We will refrain from using the term 'spanking' because it refers mostly to using a hand to inflict physical pain.

Biblical training always keeps the end goal in sight: the betterment of the child. This is the reason we like to use the word 'training'. An excellent image of comparison is the athlete who pushes (disciplines) his body so that it can accomplish what he wants it to.

---

[75] The Hebrew word *'yacar'* can mean: chastise, instruct, correct, teach, bound, punish, reform, or reprove.

He does not exhaust his body for nothing. His goals are before him just as the training of godly children is before us. We need to win.

> And everyone who competes in the games exercises self-control in all things. They then do it to receive a perishable wreath, but we an imperishable. Therefore I run in such a way, as not without aim; I box in such a way, as not beating the air; but I buffet my body and make it my slave, lest possibly, after I have preached to others, I myself should be disqualified (1 Cor 9:25-27).

The word for buffet means to beat, treat roughly and discipline by hardships. The athlete is willing to go to such extremes so that he can win a temporary prize. In a similar way, the parent wants the child to mature, thus the parents are willing to undergo any pain and sacrifice necessary to see that maturity develop. The pain is a small price to pay for the eternal reward of a well-trained child that loves God and others.

Discipline, the infliction of physical pain, is a significant part of training our children. Raising children without discipline is like driving a car without oil. We won't go far before we destroy the whole car. We have a choice: do it right and cause our children to be blessings, or ignore God's instruction in His Word and end up with an uncontrollable child.

We hope that our children would act good enough not to need physical discipline, but all of our children, by their sinful nature, will reveal a need for more than just a good talking-to.

Some parents do not like the idea of physical discipline because it reminds them of the many abuses they have either heard about or experienced. We grieve with those who have suffered so. These stained images of discipline do not help. However, if a parent lives in fear of disciplining the wrong way, this attitude will cause the parent to neglect discipline in the end.

Other parents end up lashing out at their children after frustration and anger have built up. They might hit their child to keep some form of personal sanity. In other words, the parents do not inflict pain upon the child to help the child, but only to vent their own anger and satiate their personal need for peace and quiet. It's no wonder that parents and children alike are so confused about discipline, and that many disregard it altogether.

Another kind of parent might think she is being kind or loving by overlooking the many small incidents of disobedience. Unfortunately, she has set herself up for big frustration because, by allowing the child to continue to disobey, that parent is in fact training the child to disobey! In this case, the parent should have disciplined the child when he disobeyed the first time.

The parent could have then disciplined the child without the pent up anger and agitation that she later exhibited. The parent would also be focusing on training the child to obey rather than to disobey.

Discipline has two sides: instruction and correction.

Proper discipline should always be motivated by love for the child, and that love should always keep the well-being of the child and his future maturity in mind. The parents need to genuinely care for the child; in so caring, the parents will consistently correct him. We might think our feelings show us a better way, but they will betray us. If our feelings tell us to overlook his bad behavior, or make excuses for his undisciplined condition, does that not reveal a desire to preserve the parents' own comfort? If the parent is unwilling to confront the sin in his child, perhaps it is because the parent cares more about himself than the child.

At times, we will need to strike our child hard, but we need not fear. It will not hurt him for long. In fact, it will bring long-term help to the child. Of course, we must be careful not to bruise or tear the child's skin. A small fresh branch (this is what a rod is) with rough spots smoothed over) enables us to bring a brief sting of pain without any damage. If you need any confidence, just take a good look at children who are not disciplined; they are proud, unruly, mouthy, out of control, and quick to hurt others.

The Advantages of Discipline

The advantages of discipline are many and far-reaching. A parent can positively affect a child's life through good training, and will later reap the beautiful reward of well-trained children and the relationships that that training can bring.

Advantages of Discipline	
Discipline your son while there is hope, And do not desire his death. (Proverbs 19:18)	Discipline brings hope into the life of a child.
Cease listening, my son, to discipline, And you will stray from the words of knowledge. (Proverbs 19:27)	Our willingness to accept correction and our ability to learn is closely related.
Train up a child in the way he should go, Even when he is old he will not depart from it. (Proverbs 22:6)	Parents can influence how a child should live by the training that they provide.
My son, let them not depart from your sight; Keep sound wisdom and discretion, (Proverbs 3:21)	The father's words of instruction enable a child to live a good healthy life.

A father's instruction forms a wall of protection around the child that brings long-lasting support. The father's wisdom is passed on to the child, which in time becomes the child's wisdom. He should not need to experiment with things to test their value.

The Consequences of the Lack of Discipline	
Discipline your son while there is hope, And do not desire his death. (Proverbs 19:18)	Early death is associated with undisciplined children.
The rod and reproof give wisdom, ... (Proverbs 29:15)	Physical correction must be given along with words of rebuke to bring forth wisdom.
... But a child who gets his own way brings shame to his mother. (Proverbs 29:15)	A parent that gives into the child's demands will receive shame.
Discipline your son while there is hope, And do not desire his death. (Proverbs 19:18)	Discipline brings hope into the life of a child.

Without proper and consistent discipline, a child will persist in his foolish ways. He will assume that he deserves the very best treatment from others, which can cause him to become proud. In order to get what he thinks he should receive, he will fight and argue. He disregards authorities and is only focused on himself. Because of this, he will encounter negative repercussions and, without changes to his behavior, harsh consequences.

Parent/Child Relationships

Correct your son, and he will give you comfort; He will also delight your soul. (Proverbs 29:17)	The way to build a good relationship with your child is to correct him.
A wise son makes a father glad, But a foolish man despises his mother. (Proverbs 15:20)	A foolish child does not esteem his parents.
My son, do not reject the discipline of the LORD, Or loathe His reproof, for whom the LORD loves He reproves, Even as a father, the son in whom he delights. (Proverbs 3:11-12)	Parents who discipline their children really know what it means to love them.

The parents' relationship with their child is clearly addressed in Proverbs. On one hand, if a child is corrected, he will live a sweet life with his parents. The parents will be able to continue to enjoy their relationship with their child, despite the challenges of growing up. There will be no angst or rebellion between the child and the parents.

On the other hand, without consistent discipline, the child will reject his parents. As much as the parents try, they will not gain his confidence because he despises them in his heart.

The rod is used to associate a stinging pain with sin. The pain is short and quick, which allows space for the relationship between parent and child to be immediately straightened out. The branch or switch cuts down a child's pride and allows him to regain a proper attitude toward God and his parents. We find that within five minutes, an entire situation can return to normal, whether it be a problem of disrespecting the parent or fighting with his brother.

After any tears, the child is trained to state what he/she did wrong, apologize, and hug.

The Use of a Rod in Physical Correction	
He who spares his rod hates his son, ... (Proverbs 13:24)	A rod is used in the process of discipline.
Foolishness is bound up in the heart of a child; The rod of discipline will remove it far from him. (Proverbs 22:15)	The rod of discipline is an effective tool to frustrate the foolishness of children.

Spanking (by the hand) is often ineffective because it does not sting. If one spanks on a bare bottom, it might sting, but our purpose in discipline is not to embarrass but to inflict short pain. The scriptures do not speak of methods other than the rod so it ought not to be neglected when physical discipline is necessary.

Conclusion

The differences between a child who has received discipline and a child who has not are astounding. God has clearly spoken in His Word about how to train children. When the culture erodes or perverts a man's sense of responsibility to train his children, then society itself will degenerate. God rejects any method of child training that does not include discipline or physical pain. Discipline with a rod plays a key role in the training children need to become responsible adults.

Training at Different Stages in Life

Training and its necessary arm of discipline take on different forms during the various stages of a child's life and growth. The goals, however, do not change. There is also an important continuity between the different levels of training; in order to transition smoothly in toddler training, training must begin early in the baby's life.

1) Infants to five months: Adjustments

The child at this stage of life is both physically and emotionally immature. Although only an infant, he is still capable of expressing his sinful nature. He is born with a bent to fulfill his desires. This foolishness can be seen in his persistence in trying to get his own way. The one way a baby can express his foolishness to his parents is through his cry.

An infant has needs and the only means of expressing them is crying. That is the way God designed it. They cannot talk yet, or make intentional movements, so crying and fussing is their only means of communication. Because of this, unless a parent is aware and paying attention to the child's needs, it can BECOME manipulation in very little time. It may start out as an expression of a need, with the baby getting proper attention. But when this happens a few times, the baby will catch on. It can easily get to a point where there are no needs, just wants and cries to fulfill those wants. This is the beginning stage of how a baby learns to call the shots. It is much better for parents to lead by paying attention and anticipating the baby's needs. A good routine helps immensely in this process, as parents learn about their new baby.

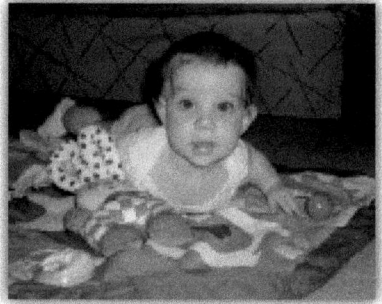

Three Training Areas

Discipline & Training of Small Children   167

There are three areas of training to focus on at this age: feeding, awake time, and sleep time. These are just about the only things a newborn will do. The first thing to note here is that a switch is not necessary at this stage. A baby cannot understand instruction. Without clear instruction, then there is no disobedience. The rod will come in handy later when the child begins to understand instruction.

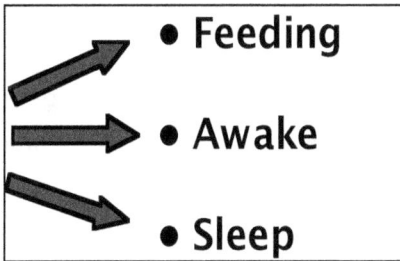

- **Feeding**
- **Awake**
- **Sleep**

The infant, however, is trained by use of constraint. We simply do not allow the baby to get his own way; instead, as parents, we dictate the schedule of the child in order that he might have stability and assurance, knowing that things happen as the parent decides.

This might sound cruel, but it is not. The child does not know right from wrong, what he may or may not do. He learns by experimentation. If the results are pleasing, then he will do it again. It's as simple as disallowing him to do the things that we do not want him to do, and instead positively reinforce the things we do want him to do. Of course, we cannot restrain his crying, so instead we need to make sure that we do not reinforce his crying response by giving him what he wants willy-nilly. Let us provide a few examples from each of the three areas of an infant's life.

Feeding

The mother should not allow the child to hit her when feeding. If a child is prone to this, constraining the flailing arms is a good way to reinforce that hitting is not allowed. Although the way the baby flings his arms might look cute at first, we know in the long run that it can be dangerous, or at least troublesome. What the parent does not like, the parent does not tolerate. The mother can simply hold one or both of the baby's hands while using her other hand to feed.

The parent also should not feed the baby every time he cries. Often, a baby will cry because he wants warmth and comfort. This is not wrong in and of itself, but you must note that it will lead to manipulation even when the baby is doing fine. Although a feeding might provide that extra comfort, we are giving into the wrong demands of the child. With scheduled feedings, the mom sets the routine, though this cannot usually be worked out until a month or so after birth, and even then, there is much that can interrupt a good routine.

Awake time

Children typically love to be held. At first, the child's playtime will be very limited. Infants often don't stay awake very long. When they are awake, they are often being held. But parents must be diligent to find a time in the routine when they put the baby down to play. It might be in a playpen, bassinet, or on a blanket. Again the baby might cry to be held. He is used to the mother's warmth. If he does cry, check that he is not dirty or wet, and make sure that play time is not so close to nap time; it's okay to let him squirm and fuss a bit.

He will soon learn that there is no reward for his crying. Instead he will learn to be content by himself. We only would caution you not leave him there for long. Don't make it so that he needs to cry to get your attention. Otherwise, you will run into the same problem you're trying to solve. In this case, we'd be conditioning him to cry in order to be picked up. Routines help so much at this stage.

Sleeping

When it comes to sleep, a mother ought to ensure that her child is sleepy and ready to nap with a clean diaper and full tummy.

When everything is in order, a mother can put her child in his bed and let him cry, since she's already made sure that everything else is taken care of.

The baby may have some extra frustration and need to cry it out. When cried out (usually a few minutes), he will contentedly go to sleep. We should not let the child get his way of getting in a more comfortable position (such as the mother's arms) just because he wants to. The mother either needs her own rest or has other work to do. Again, it is not appropriate to spank a baby for crying; he can cry. Let him wear himself out for a few minutes and he will most likely sleep.

2) Six to Twelve Months: Mobile

The child typically starts to crawl around six months and begins to walk around one year. There is no need to worry if they start a few months earlier or later because every child is unique. The difference between this stage and the first is that the young child is beginning to be mobile. The child will first learn to reach, roll over, and aim for distant objects. In other words, they can begin to get into things.

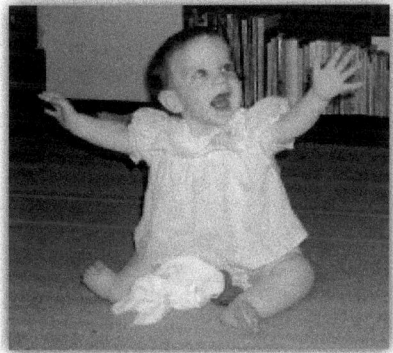

Children are so delightful at this stage, with their fascination with toys and their reactions to people. At the same time, however, we must remember that their sinful nature is developing and seeking ways to express itself.

As long as the child is immobile, he is well protected. The only things the child can reach are things they are allowed to touch. We do not put them near dangerous things or items that belong to others. As they begin to roll and crawl, however, they begin to maneuver themselves into places where there are things they shouldn't touch, and so you have a decision to make. You could move the objects that are off-limits, but in doing so, the child has not learned how to respect the parents' "no." At this stage, you should begin to train the child to obey your word.

Early on, you can say "No" and thump his hand with your index finger when he snatches your glasses. Or, if while holding the baby on your lap at the table he reaches to grab a plate or some other item, you need only say, "No" and constrain the child's arm or thump him with your index finger. You are familiarizing him with the word 'no' and restraint. The baby needs to learn that there are some things that are off limits.

If we let them play with anything that they can reach, it will only be a few months until the house is totally rearranged! If we allow our children to touch whatever they can, we'd end up putting every hazardous or meaningful object out of reach. In my living room, there is a wood stove that gets very hot during the winter. We once asked a group of parents how they would deal with a child that was just starting to crawl. One suggested that we not use the stove, while another suggested that we put up a barricade all the way across the room! Others said that they would always supervise their child. As far as I can recollect, no one suggested simply training the child not to touch it!

How do we train the mobile child?

Remember that having constrained the child at an earlier age, he will realize that some things are not okay. The child will already have learned to associate the word 'no' with certain things that they are not allowed to do. Now you need to take a few more steps. At this point it is okay to start using the rod when the child is mobile and can understand instruction.

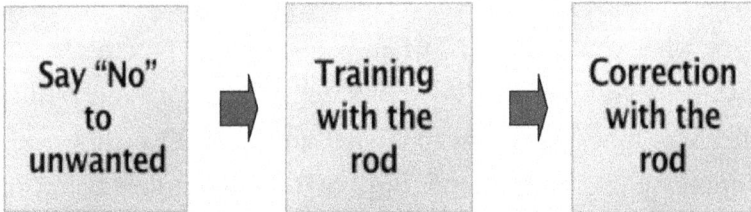

Say "No" to unwanted	⇒	Training with the rod	⇒	Correction with the rod

THE TRAINING PROCESS

For example, if we tell the child 'no' to touching something, we should see him withdraw his hand. As is typical though, we might also see the child go to touch it again when he thinks we are not watching. We must train the child to associate the sting of the rod with the word 'no.' The child is small, only crawling. We are using the switch for training along with our 'no' and a tap on their little hand that is enough to make it sting. They will quickly catch on.

Once the child touches the things that Dad or Mom say 'no' to, they will get a slight, unpleasant tap on their hand. The goal is that they learn to obey your verbal instruction (your "no") without the switch, which should primarily be used as a reinforcement at this stage.

I remember a time that I wanted to keep our nine-month-old in my study. I used our switch as the boundary and slapped it on the floor so she could hear it and associate it as such. The first few times she got close to the line, I reminded her not to cross it by repeating that sound and saying 'no.' I only had to tap her once or twice for crossing the line. And I mean tap, too. In fact, when I said 'no,' she began to react with tears because her own way was frustrated.

Your "no" should be delivered with a pleasant voice and smile. You want to condition your child to respond to your smile, not your frown. Make sure you mean 'no' when you say it. Your child must learn to trust your word. As the saying goes, "Mean what you say and say what you mean." If, when you say "no," he cries, and you relent and give him what he wants, what has that taught him? It teaches him that crying gets him what he wants. The same goes for whining, pouting, or any other display of unacceptable behavior or attitude.

Picking up toys

A child should learn to pick up after himself. Some parents still pick up after their teenager. Why? It is not because the parent likes to do so! It's because they neglected to train him when he was very little. The child needs to realize that he is responsible for his own actions.

A child will go through several short phases as he matures at this point in his life.

(1) The first phase is coming to understand order. When a baby can sit up and observe what is around him, the parent should first restore order to the toys around the child before taking him away from the crib or playpen. Whenever "playpen time" was over, my wife made sure it was nice and orderly before taking the baby out. While neatening up she would say things like "clean-up time" or "let's make this place nice and neat," or would instruct the child to "put that toy here, that toy there." It's important to talk about what you are doing. This can be a game at first. There is no need for disciplinary action or harsh words, either. Speak excitedly, "Put away time!" The child will only have a positive attitude toward cleaning up.

(2) In the following phase, the parent will simply need to guide the child's hands to help him put the objects away one by one. The two phases can merge together nicely; the first shows him, and the second helps him.

(3) Later, in this last phase, the child will do it by himself. It won't take long for the child to become acquainted with this routine. The parents' role is to remind, at this stage. As the child grows, there will be attached consequences for not picking up as told.

Changing the diaper

No one likes changing diapers, and the way a baby can squirm and roll over makes the task much more difficult! We know of situations where two adults were needed to change one baby's diaper! Linda used (and now uses for grandchildren) a foolproof method to minimize the squirming.

If she notices any movement, she gives verbal instruction "No, lay still," and then with her left hand holds the baby's feet and lightly plants her left elbow in the middle of the baby's tummy as she changes him with her right hand. Now the baby knows to associate Linda's "no" with restraint. It is that easy.

Feeding

At around six months, babies usually start to eat solids. Many parents are preoccupied with what the baby eats. In this section we talk about training a baby to eat. Here we are faced with the question: Who is training whom?

Since the child does not know right from wrong, clean from dirty, good habit from bad, it's important that a parent teach the child what is acceptable and unacceptable behavior during mealtime. If the parent starts off right, future meal training will be simpler.

For example, when a parent is feeding a child, they don't want the child to intercept the spoon. There is food on it, and the child will likely make a mess. The baby is too young to feed himself; he just isn't coordinated. The easiest way to keep him from making a mess is for the mother to give verbal instruction "put your hands down" and at the same time to hold his hands with one of hers and use the other to feed.

Although this might sound terribly constraining, remember that, if you start early on, the child won't know it is constraint. If he learns to eat that way, he will consider it normal to have his hands held away from the food. How does this help the child in the long run? He is learning self-control. He is learning what food is for (eating not playing); he is learning to yield to authority.

The child learns to accept the restriction of his freedom as normal. If done from the beginning, he doesn't know any different. He expects it. Before long, you will be able to take your hands off the child's hands, and he will keep his hands off the food. It really works, and is easier than you think. Parents simply have no confidence that they can do it or any idea that they should.

I still remember when we were going through this process with one of our daughters. She was very active and had a hard time keeping still. When her hands were held, she learned to accept that. When Linda began to take her hands off of hers, our daughter didn't keep her hands folded down as we suggested but high in the air, waving back and forth. This was fine for us because ultimately she kept her hands in the air away from the food, which was our goal.

3) Toddlers: Walking and Dangerous

Whenever toddlers begin to walk, their hands will reach for whatever they desire. They can walk, climb, and jump now. They can bring their hands to the objects they want to touch. They need to very clearly learn limits or they will quickly find themselves in a lot of danger.

Some parents do not understand training at all. They believe that the only way to protect the child is to be with the child on a 24-hour watch. I am amazed to see how dutiful these parents can be. On the other hand, they are just putting off the danger because there will be a point when the child will learn to operate behind their parents' back. They still wouldn't have learned to control themselves to do what is right.

Once a child has learned the power of the word 'no' in association with a tap with the rod, everything else will follow. When appropriate, we need to go where the child can go and clearly instruct them in what is off limits. Although we might feel there are some items a child could touch but not play with, such as a lamp, it is best to have them not touch those objects at all. Clear instructions are important.

Take the child to a room and point out everything that is off-limits. Point out the lamps, forbid climbing on bookcases, touching certain knobs and remote controls, etc. As you point out each item, you should have your switch in hand and knock it a few times against the floor or something hard so they hear the sound and are reminded of the sting of the rod. One object after another, point and instruct him. Afterwards, watch him play for a few minutes. He might be tempted to touch some of the things that he is not supposed to touch. At the beginning, just state a clear 'no' as he approaches a forbidden object. If he persists in touching that object, use the switch to sting his hand to remind him clearly that that object is off-limits.

How hard?

The tap that you used when he was six months is not going to be as effective when he is two years old. How hard do you sting? I first practice on myself so that I am sensitive to its pain. Do remember that every child is different. Some children are more sensitive than others, while others are hardly dazed with a firm swat. You can gauge a child's sensitivity by observing them when you use the rod. We need to strike them hard enough to sting; if it is too soft, the child will become defiant, adopting an attitude as though he has beaten the beast. Instead of defiance, we should see a humbled heart and change of attitude. If I miscalculate the firmness, and he ends up with a defiant spirit, I warn him of my observations and that it will be worse next time. Sometimes the warning works, but often the child will need to be chastised again within a few hours.

The phrase "terrible twos" is an oft-heard phrase, and is used by some parents to characterize the open defiance of their two-year-olds; they are shocked at some of the things their child says or does. This stage begins with the slow realization that they can exercise their own will, that they have power to make decisions. It is the awakening of their self-awareness. They see that they can control their mouth and will. In a sense, they have identified their own person. Now they can expertly exert their foolishness if given the opportunity. Of course, the parents who have not trained their children will face a little monster. Children manipulate their parents through their cries, actions, mean words, and temper tantrums, a false sense of being hurt, "tiredness," "pain," and a lot of other things.

This is not to say that a trained child will not also discover his own will. You will have a few months when he expresses this defiance, but it won't be anything too spectacular because he has already been conditioned by your words, the switch, and a regular routine. The parent might be shocked at having to use the rod so frequently on their once well-trained child, but they should not be disturbed. Stay on the path and discipline that you've already established and remember to use the rod hard enough to make a difference. You will soon not need it as much and your 'no' will be sufficient.

When the switch is used in the right way, it reminds the child that he cannot always get what he wants. It associates the pain of the sting with their disobedience. They find that it is preferable to refrain from some naughty action than to feel the sting of discipline. This is true with getting dressed, eating, going to sleep, going to the bathroom, etc. There must be a consistent enforcement of the rules at this stage because the child is learning to exert his will. They will test everything they can think of.

We should remember, however, that a child at this stage will do things that we have not clearly instructed them on. We have wasted quite a bit of toilet paper when our little one discovered that it will keep coming off the roll. Guess what? It became another "no, off limits" object once it was discovered. We need to remember to distinguish between childishness and rebellion. Childishness is when a child does things that are improper yet doesn't know it because there was

no clear instruction. Rebellion is when they know it is wrong and still do it.[76]

Training has everything going for it. It works for you when you have the child eat, put things away, or start potty training. Let's discuss a few of these items here.

Feeding the child

Perhaps one of the most stressful moments in training is teaching your child to feed himself. It's paired with so much frustration that there are families who take up their dining room carpet or simply put this training off until the child is much older. However, the parents should begin to train the child when he is sufficiently coordinated and begins to show an interest in the process, which is usually around 15 months.

You might think the previous constraint-training is difficult (holding his hands), but once you see how it prepares the child to eat properly by himself, then you might think differently. Training becomes a pleasant endeavor when the rebellious heart of the child is suppressed. Everyone will be able to enjoy themselves around the table. Every parent will face the foolish heart of the child. When the child is not under control, we can understand why parents might not give their child the freedom to feed himself, instead continuing to treat the little boy or girl like a baby. However, the toddler is no longer a baby. He needs to be treated as a responsible little boy or girl. The child would also benefit from the use of all of his newly acquired motor skills.

When the child realizes that he is not to touch or play with food, he accepts that as normal. So Mom will eventually be able to release the child's hands and the child will not play with the food. Because of this training, the child will appreciate the opportunity to eat

[76] We thank Gary Ezzo for making this distinction really clear.

certain finger foods. Later he will enjoy the challenge of learning to eat with a spoon. Let's be more specific about how to do this.

At around fifteen months (ages differ), the child will be able to begin to eat on his own. There are two aspects of feeding himself that will need to be paid attention to. The first is the spoon-to-mouth action, and the latter is the dig action.

The child will first learn how to bring his spoon to his mouth. We suggest start the training at the end of a meal. When he only has a few bites left, give him a spoon and properly place it in his hand. The parent will put food on the spoon and then guide the child's hand, on the spoon, to the mouth. This of course only works if the child has learned to accept the parent's guidance. The child will quickly want to lift the spoon by himself, but the parent will still need to put food on the spoon for him.

The time will soon come when the child wants to put the food on the spoon himself. Again, start at the end of the meal. He might get more interested in the process than the food. Give him something that is easier to pick up, like applesauce or pudding or something sticky. And, again, guide his hand. The child will learn to both gather food on his spoon and feed himself. A little guidance from the parent goes a long way in training the child.

But what if the child accidentally spills foods? Accidents should be cleaned up cheerfully and quickly forgotten. We can certainly caution them "Be careful." If, after he has mastered this skill, and he purposely spills or makes a mess, he should have his hand tapped and then be made to help clean up. Some of your verbal instruction could include things like: "We must be careful not to waste the good food God has given us," or "It is not good to make work for someone else."

What if the child experiments with feeding the floor? "Spoon overboard!" Well, it will happen, but we need to distinguish between childishness and disobedience. The first time it happens is truly an honest experiment. We tell the child a calm, "No." Mention that if he does it again that you will need to use the rod. Sometimes it helps to put the rod within eyesight, which is a good reminder for why he should not do it. Of course, if the child puts the food on the floor, then sting him on the offending hand with the rod. If we see him regularly misbehaving, then we will simply take away the privilege (freedom) of feeding himself and return to holding his hands.

Since a child makes a bit of noise crying when disciplined, we often put the child by himself in an adjoining room rather than disturb the rest of the family meal.

Picking up

When the child is more mobile, it gets a bit more difficult to figure out how to train him to pick up after himself, but don't be discouraged!

The first thing to keep in mind is to train the child to stay in one room or play area. Let the child play with toys only there. Then it is not so difficult to train the child to clean up. Another help is to limit the number of toys that we own or have available. We have eight children and have been given a lot of toys over the years. One of the key points we trained our children in was to put away the toys they were playing with before taking others out. This training, however, needs close supervision. If you allow your child to take out too many things at once, he will have an overwhelming job at the end of his playtime. Limiting access to toys helps prevent this.

If we let the child wander around, he will make messes all over the place. Remember, the child who began training early on will be used to and even happy to pick up. Don't pick up for him. If he seems discouraged, just pick things up with him. If he gets rebellious and refuses, you might just need to take his hand and force it to pick up. This is fortunately rather rare.

Summary

We have found that a child can do far more than he is given credit for. Any parent can train their child to do anything that they are physically capable of. There are two important parts:

The constraint. We limit the ability of the child to express his own will. We only allow him to do well. The switch is a helpful tool to enforce good training.

The training. We train the child to gain the skills he needs to accomplish different tasks. The child doesn't know what to do or how to do it, so we tell him, show him, and patiently guide him at first until he is able and willing to do it in a pleasing way by himself.

In the next chapter, we will talk more about routines. Routines are closely associated with the training of doing the proper things at the right time. Routines provide a more comprehensive look at what needs to be done and when.

#7 Study Questions

1. How important is discipline?

2. What is the biblical word for discipline? How is it different from just the negative connotation of discipline used today?

3. What are the two parts of training?

4. What does God's Word say about the rod?

5. What does God's Word say about discipline?

6. What is the nature of the newborn like? How does he express his nature?

7. What is the nature of the toddler? How does he express it?

8. What is the purpose of training?

9. What part does instruction play in the training process?

10. What influence do parents have on the life of their child?

11. From Proverbs what are some of the consequences of no training?

12. Describe one way to train a child to feed himself.

Godly Beginnings for the Family   ROUTINES

Training & Routines for Small Children

Contrary to what you might hear, parents have a great impact on their child and the way he or she ultimately lives life. God made it this way. The parent is to *"train up the child in the way he should go."* It is the epitome of bad parenting to let the child become who he is naturally. The sin nature, along with ignorance, will lead all untrained children into ungodliness and the expression of their foolish hearts whether or not they frequent a church. Ungodliness always brings ugly consequences.

As parents, we desire to give our children a comfortable life and all the good things that God has bestowed upon us. However, by indiscriminately giving our children all the things that their little hearts desire, we are inadvertently creating a problem. By giving our children many privileges, possessions, and freedoms, they will be predisposed to becoming spoiled, and our quest to raise godly children will be frustrated. If we are not careful to train our children in the right way very early on, we are actually training him to go the wrong way.

Good parents must persevere in properly training their children. When they train their children properly, they will lessen the effects of evil. Proper training will always include both discipline and instruction. Unfortunately, some parents tend to incorporate all forms of discipline except the aspect of physical discipline. We should not be afraid to physically chastise. Notice the impact that the trouble or affliction had on this person in the following verses.

> Before I was afflicted I went astray, but now I keep Thy word (Ps 119:67).
> It is good for me that I was afflicted, that I may learn of Thy statutes (Ps 119:71).

God even uses affliction (pain, suffering, difficulty) to help us live the best life possible. Without it, we will go astray. As this is true for us, so it is true for our children. When our children learn to fear physical correction, it helps to keep them safe and develop a good attitude toward learning.

Understanding the Training Process

Let's review what we learned about discipline from the previous chapter. Discipline is often associated with keeping a child from doing something harmful or potentially dangerous. We want to keep them away from what they shouldn't touch or do. For example, we do not want our child to explore a dangling cord for fear that playing with it could bring a lamp down on top of them.

We use our verbal "no" along with a slight tap from a little branch (switch, rod) to help them obey our verbal instruction. When the child is small, there is momentary pain associated with the rod. The better a job we do, the less we will need to use it later on in life. The presence of the rod, though, will help the child comply with a parent's instruction. We will focus on how to properly instruct and train a young child in this last chapter.

The manner in which we instruct our child to do things will vary, depending on how old the child is. We just need to remember that all the things we do for them early on will become natural to them. It will become a way of life. Let me give you a simple example.

A baby about six months old is learning to use his hands to grab things. We want him to learn that there are some things that are off-limits. We know later when he is mobile, that he will pull at all sorts of things. He wants to see what happens when he pulls something. At this age, however, he is hardly conscious that he is even grabbing. It doesn't matter if he is conscious of whether it is right or wrong, harmful or helpful. But because we don't want him to do it, we are motivated to train him at this age, on this point.

If the child grabs your glasses, simply take the child's hand off the glasses and say a firm "no." The parent can then either thump the child's hand with his forefinger or tuck the child's hand under his arm so he can't move it. The child is learning that there are things that are off-limits. He does not like his hand constrained, and he will remember the negative consequences of grabbing glasses. It might take a few attempts in order for him to make the connection (it depends on how old he is), so you must be patient and train him. After a while, he will make the connection.

"No!"

At six months, a child will be easier to train. It takes a simple situation, the use of a kind voice, and a little effort to restrain his hand. But the baby learned from the repetition. What has the child learned?

- The child has learned that "no" means don't do it.
- The child has learned that there are negative consequences associated with "no."
- The child has learned that when he hears "no" and stops doing it, there are no negative consequence.
- The child, on a broader scale, is learning that there are things in this world that he is not allowed to do.
- The child learns that if he doesn't get his way, life is easier and even better (no consequence).
- The child is learning to respect and obey his authorities.

Wise parents should choose neutral (as much as possible) situations for training. The child is just being a child. But the child still needs to learn that he cannot do everything freely. At other times, the child will still insist on his own way, which requires a parent to follow up immediately. If the child is young, the parent accompanies his "no" with a thump from an index finger. Later, it will be a slight tap from a small switch. Later on, it will be a sting on his leg or hand with a longer switch that can make a nice swoosh sound.

We want to train the child to obey us the first time we give him instructions. Is this not what God wants? When we read His Word, does He not mean for us to obey at the point of instruction? Sure. So this is the way we train our own children. Proper training keeps them from the worst and provides them an opportunity to obtain the best. Now, let's see how routines fit into the young child's life.

Training Routines into the Child

God made us creatures of habit. What we are used to, we will become familiar with and tend to like and therefore repeat. A routine is a regular way of caring for a child so that the child learns how to properly conduct life on his own. By repetition we build the cycle of expectation, reward, and familiarity. Remember how we saw this in the suggested infant routine that was discussed in an earlier chapter.

ORGANIZATION HELPS THE MOTHER AND STABILIZES THE CHILD

> **feed awake sleep feed awake sleep feed awake sleep**

Note the constant, repetitive pattern here. The baby begins to expect these things and therefore learns to wait and trust. The baby learns also that he conforms to other people's schedules. These attitudes and approaches to life are the building blocks of self-control.

DISORGANIZATION CONFUSES MOTHER AND CHILD

Without the organization of her life, a child will become impulsive. The child only gets things when she cries (sometimes yells or demands) for it. If the mother doesn't come quickly, the baby will cry louder until she does. These babies are demanding and are conditioned to having others work around their own demands. This is the opposite of self-control.

In a well-organized schedule, a child will learn confidence (faith) in what should happen. They will develop expectations they can depend on. As their motor skills develop, they will gain confidence that they themselves can do the same things. They want these things to happen. They do not question whether or not to brush their teeth, take a bath, sit still to eat, pick up toys, etc., because they are already used to it. Their first ambition is to do it themselves.

Repetition
Ordered
Unified
Train
Instruct
Nice
Enforce

- **Repetition** is doing things the same way over and over again with or for the child.

- **Order** refers to the logical series of activities that connects routines.

- **Unified** is a whole series of mini-routines that are combined into one concept such as 'clean-up time.'

- **Training** speaks of the step-by-step process that, over time, will enable a child to carry out the same pattern of activities on their own.

- **Instruct** refers to the words that are used to tell the child how something should be done.

- **Nice** is the kind and patient way the parent helps meet the child's needs.

- **Enforce** reminds us of the importance of consistency in carrying out consequences.

The biggest obstacle to setting up routines is the parent. There are two kinds of difficult parents:

1) Parents who do not believe the child should be held to a routine.

We really feel for this child. The child does not learn to live by faith in what should be, but by what they want. They are desire oriented. That is, they only know how to get things that they want when the want them. They do not know how to do what is expected of them. If something is demanded of them, they put up a fuss. The parent learns to bribe them with a sweet or other reward to do what they want. This child has no self-control (in the sense of doing what is right or proper).

2) Parents who do not believe a child can be trained.

This parent simply does not believe the child can be trained. Since they believe that they can't be trained, the parent makes no effort to try. The parent has no faith (confidence) in the process or in the child. Therefore, the child never learns. Sometimes the child wants to do things for himself, but the parent doesn't have confidence in the child.

If any parent wants to learn how, they can train their child to do virtually anything that is age-appropriate. Their mental, emotional, and motor skills need to mature to a certain level to accomplish different activities. Some parents want their child to do something like crawling or talking early. Every child will naturally develop these skills; the parent can waste a lot of time trying to give the child a "head start." We are not talking about this kind of training. The child learns these things at the appropriate time.

Feeding, waking, and sleeping times are the first main areas of training. The baby needs to be trained because they will attempt to frustrate the best routine to satisfy their own desires, if allowed. We have talked about some of these things in previous chapters. Our teaching focuses on how to keep them from doing wrong. Go back and read it if you have forgotten. We will focus on instructions for carrying out specific tasks here.

Routines and Tasks

Each routine is made up of a number of tasks and goals. Always use a pleasant voice when talking to your child about various routines. Verbalize what you are doing. Let's look at some examples. Each discussion will start young and progress.

a) **Brushing teeth**

When a child's first tooth comes in, it is time to start the tooth brushing routine. When very little still, it is easy for the mother to quickly clean those few teeth, and as teeth come in more abundantly, a brush will be used. The mother is to take the baby and hold him or her as she brushes the existing teeth. The baby might fuss, but the mother needs simply to tell the baby "no" and hold the baby's hands. The child will get used to this.

When the child begins to get older, it will be obvious that the child will want to try brushing his own teeth. The regular routine has allowed him to build in this expectation and has given him the desire to be part of fulfilling it (to be like a grown-up). The parent needs to gradually release the restraint. We won't allow the child to brush their teeth all at once because they cannot do a proper job yet. Once they get the idea that they can do it, it is hard to convince them otherwise. They will demand full freedom and you will have a regular struggle.

Instead you need to take calculated steps. When the child looks able and begins to signal his interest, you can begin allowing them to handle their tooth brush and guide him in "brushing" his teeth. Of course, he cannot do a good job at this point; you're simply allowing him to start practicing. Step-by-step you will give the child the opportunity to take part in all of the "tooth brushing" opportunities. The full tooth brushing routine includes: going to the bathroom, reaching the brush, getting a small cup of water, wetting the brush a bit, putting a tiny bit of toothpaste on the brush, putting the tube cover back, brushing correctly, spitting out the toothpaste, taking a little drink of water to rinse mouth, rinsing off the toothbrush, putting the toothbrush away in its proper place, putting the cup back and leaving the room for what is next.

The child just crawling or walking cannot do all this at first. Step-by-step we train with him. By the time our children were about five years old, they were able to do all of this well, except maybe reaching and putting away their toothbrushes. It is a process. We did it with the child, step-by-step, until they reached the point of ability. Then they were able to completely take over the mini-routine. We could say that it was time to brush their teeth, and off they went. When the child is finally able to do the job, he should be given the full responsibility to do it on his own.

b) Putting Clothes Away

First, clarify the goal. We want the child to be able to put away his or her clothes properly after use.

Dirty clothes

Dirty clothes are easy to take care of. Once the child can walk, they love to help deliver things. The first few times, the mother should accompany the child with the dirty clothes and drop them where needed. The problem in this case is helping the child to determine what is dirty. The child might start moving other clothes and things into the dirty pile! This can be avoided if you train the child to put the clothes away right after they take them off.

Folding Clothes

What about clothes that will be worn again, such as pajamas? We should think about this routine along with its timing. For example, in the case of pajamas, he will first learn to take his pajamas off when he gets up and then properly put them away after he is dressed.

Folding pajamas might seem difficult, but again it is not hard because the child sees it being done every day. When the child gets up in the morning, get them dressed and then right away fold the pajamas and put them away while they remain with you. As the child is able and seems motivated to start helping in the process, the parent will help him start folding his own clothes. Perhaps the first part would be for us to fold it and then encouragingly say, "Go put your pajamas under your pillow" or wherever you designate. They will be proud of their work.

As a next step, you child will show his desire to help you fold his pajamas. Perhaps at first the parent can do the first folds and just save the last one for the child. Guide the little one's hand to make the last fold. Then have him put his pajamas away. As his skills develop, he will do more of the folds with your guidance, and as he learns to do a fold, we excitedly say, "Now your turn to fold. Can you do it?" They will do it. If they get frustrated, say something like, "Whoops," or "Let's do it together," and then take his hand and guide it to do it right.

The child will soon learn to be able to do it all by himself. He will be proud of his accomplishments. This is the full "put away pajamas" routine. Now we need to make sure they do it consistently every day. Don't let them get sloppy (putting the pajamas away without folding) or neglectful (not doing it). The excitement at some point will wear off and they might refuse to do it. But we can rest assured in the knowledge that they are trained. We usually only need to remind them of the rod, which is usually enough for them to gain extra motivation right away in ninety percent of the cases and do it properly. If they still refuse, then we need to use the rod by slapping it across their legs with a little sting.

This "fold your pajamas" sub-routine will soon become part of a larger "getting up in the morning" routine. Let's look at another aspect of this bigger routine.

c) Getting Dressed

The goal is to train the children to dress themselves without being told. This is more complex and requires longer training.

Repetition is key in this training. The mother needs to be with the child when he wakes up. At that point you must help him undress. The child has been learning all along how to cooperate when Mom helps take off his clothes. The same will be true when they are getting dressed; the child will learn to straighten out his arm so Mom can easily put it through the sleeve. When they start doing helpful movements, encourage them with a nice compliment like "Wow, I didn't know you could do that!"

The child will learn to take off his pajamas on his own

more quickly than to put them on. Once he gets dressed, you need to train him automatically to find his pajamas, fold them, and put them away. Getting dressed will require much more skill development.

Summer clothes are easier to learn to put on. The main point is, parents must first do all of the dressing. The child watches and will then be able to help with one or two items. Sooner or later, if we lay out the underwear for the child flat on the floor, the child can put them on correctly. We work with them and let them do what they can. We help guide their hands to do new things and then do what they cannot do, like buttons, zippers, and belts.

Let me backtrack to infant training for a minute. The mother must establish a dressing routine that she follows, day by day. Dress the baby in the same place, put things on him in the same order, dress at the same time each day, (i.e. always before breakfast or whenever you decide).

d) The morning, or waking, routine

So we start training them in the mini-routines (putting pants on) so they can complete the subroutine (get dressed) so that they can complete the morning routine (getting ready for the day) by themselves. The parent is to determine exactly what is included in this routine. We have suggested a guideline below. Do they wake up by alarm, by the parent's call, or on their own? The parents must decide. We should leave very few decisions at this stage to the child's wants.

- **Wake up** (How does the child wake up?)
- **Get up** (How much time to actually get out of bed?)
- **Make Bed** (Making the bed satisfactorily.)
- **Dress** (Putting on the right clothes the right way.)

• **Put away clothes** (Putting away bed clothes and dirty laundry.)

• **Hygiene** (Toilet, brush teeth and hair, wash face).

There are other routines too. Some of the examples will include obvious things like a toy pick up routine, eating, or washing up. Notice the above diagram on the right.

Some items we might tend to neglect. This might be how to welcome Daddy home or how to say goodbye to Dad and Mom when they go out for the evening. We can eliminate a lot of conflict when we proactively think about these routines.

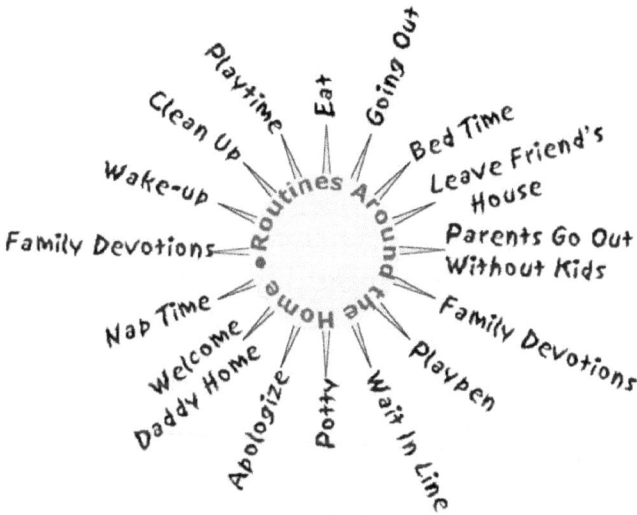

Proactive Training

When you detect areas that your children need training in, you should try to bring the training into a neutral setting. A neutral setting means a situation in which there is no parent-child confrontation. In other words, when we spot a difficult problem that needs focused attention, we will carry it out at some other time when the issue isn't up front.

1) Training to arrive without fussing

If we are going to train our child how to leave a friend's home, it is best not to train them at their friend's house. We would first do it at home. How? Let's think about it. Maybe after a little investigation, you discover three main things that your child does that you don't like:

• Takes a toy and wants to bring it home

• Refuses to help pick up what he played with

• Cries when leaving to go home

Once you determine where the chief problem is, you should first train him, at home, how to do it properly. This doesn't mean everything will go smoothly when leaving his friend's house, but it will help a lot. We know what to say to the child and how to further our training later. Meanwhile, the child is learning what to expect and how to respond.

In order to avoid whining and problems when leaving a friend's house, we verbally go through the routine with the child before we go, helping him to anticipate his forthcoming response.

If the child has siblings at home, the child will have more opportunities to practice at home because there are inter-relationship issues. They will have to learn to share toys with their brothers and sisters. They will see their siblings share toys. But the parents still need to proactively train the child.

Train to give up a toy

Plan a time you will practice with them what you would like them to do when they need to give up a toy or book. The parent makes up a game to train the child on a day when things are going well. Let's assume the child can walk. He can go over to a corner and pick up some toy or object.

The parent will tell the young child where a ball is. The child will go get it and then bring and give it to the parent. So Daddy and Mommy play this "game" with their child. In it, the child is associating the giving up of a toy with fun. The fun is the reward. Explain to the child that when they go to a friend's house, they will need to give up the toy in their hands. But don't spend too much time on the last thought. Just do it several times. Before you go over to the friend's house, remember to remind the child that if he has a toy in his hand, that he needs to give it back before he goes home.

Train to put away toys

If we have trained our child to pick up toys at home, then they should not have a problem picking up toys away from home. But several problems can occur. The host parent might be polite and say, "There is no need to pick up" which miscommunicates the need to our child. We should pick up after ourselves. Or the other parents have never trained their child to pick up and doesn't expect our child to do so either.

The child might not know where things go in somebody else's house. We need to help them find out where things go so they can put them away. Or they just might be overwhelmed if the whole room is a mess. I think this is a parental problem rather than a child problem. We cannot expect our child to pick all that mess up. We will ask our child to pick up a portion of the mess.

Training a child to pick up toys at home is a process. We were more specific in the previous lesson. Start training the child from a very early age and they will know no difference. We first make everything neat around them. Second, when older, we take their hand and put things away. Third, we allow them to put them away. Fourth, we tell them it is "pick up time" so that they know to put things away. Usually, if we train them at home, we only need to say, "Pick up time" and the child will just follow that routine.[77] Every toy should have its designated place.

Train to return home without a fuss

When it's time to go home, a child may cry. The parents should not give into the child's demands to stay. This only makes it worse next time. If the child knows that fussing gives him ten more minutes, then they will fuss for another ten minutes at every opportunity. We need to train them so that when it is time to go home, they go without a fuss.

For example, we include different steps in our training: (1) a warning that we will be leaving in five minutes, (2) expectation to pick up what they were playing with (this should not be a whole room as they only play with one thing at a time, then clean up), (3) parent's entry to see if there's any need for help, (4) the parent's compliment and then (5) guiding the child toward the doorway leading the child to be polite in saying thank you.

It is helpful to tell the other parent about your training so that the parent does not help your child get his way when he says or motions that he wants to stay longer. Let's look at another example.

2) **Training to ask nicely (sign language)**

One of the key areas children need training in is their attitude. Many parents get very frustrated because they do not know what to do with that mean face or stubborn look. "They didn't do anything

---

[77] I once showed my 2+ daughter how she could help pick up the room by helping her dolly do it. At first I asked her to put a piece of paper on the floor, but then suggested that the dolly pick it up. I went down with the doll hands and grasped that piece of paper–with lots of fun and noise–and then made imaginary steps over to the basket, and we dropped it in. She loved it and started using the dolly to help her pick up. We need to think up fun ways to train what is right.

bad." We simply need to explain to our children that we do not accept bad attitudes. If they are older, you can explain how God looks at our heart. But with a younger child, your words will not be understood.

The parents should be consistent in communicating through polite language. Does Dad say "Thank you" for dinner? Does Mom say "Please" when asking a child to do her a favor? Do Dad and Mom use nice voices when speaking polite words? Children do learn through example. But if we fool them for a while, later they will know the secret and become bitter and resentful toward us (call us a hypocrite). We are kind and treat people politely because people are made in God's image.

We have formerly discussed in another chapter how a child will try to use his cry to manipulate the parent. Remember though that if a child employs this method of manipulation, it is not the end but only the beginning! If he is successful in getting his way, the child will learn to use his whine to get what he wants. But even if the parents have not given into the baby's manipulative cry, they still might be tempted to give into the baby's whine. A child often uses his whine to get legitimate things. At that point it might not have any negative attitude with it, but it is rather unbecoming.

In order to avoid whining, we suggest that the parents teach the child a few simple sign language gestures to cultivate politeness before they can talk. The children may be too young to speak, but they do understand many things. The sign that we use for "Please" is a small circle traced on the chest. The sign for "Thank you" is to touch your lips with the front of the fingers of your right hand (with an open palm) and smile as you move your hand away, palm upward. You can find more examples on the internet.

Maybe you wonder how to teach your child sign language. It is not hard at all especially if you have trained the child to accept correction and instruction from you. They love to learn things. When the child wants something, we train them to say "Please" first. Of course, they can't say it so we say the word and simultaneously take their hand in ours and draw a circle on their chest. They very quickly learn to associate the sign with the word. More importantly, they are putting in their lives something they do when they are asking for something. If children are able to sit up, we can train them to do this.

The child will need to learn that a parent will sometimes say "Yes" and sometimes "No." But they have learned the main lesson early on when they heard you say "No" to different things and restrained their hand. Using sign language helps us to train in a better way. We can avoid much whining. If they start whining to get a drink of juice, the parent can simply remind them, "How do you ask?" and the child will sign "Please" on their chest.

3) Handling Bad Attitudes

How do we handle bad attitudes? What do we do when we tell our 1 1/2 year old to put something down, but he meanly or stubbornly throws it down? He did what we asked, didn't he? Yes and no. We must explain that his particular attitude is not acceptable in our home at any time. He put the object down, but he did it wrongly. I find it helpful to act out the two ways we can put it down.

- I make a stubborn face and throw something down.
- I happily say "Thank you" and put it down nicely.

Later on, we could play a training game. But at that point we should just instruct him how to do it with a right attitude. We tell him the right words to say. Yes, the child probably cannot say them, but he can say it in his own way. Or better, give him a sign for "Okay Daddy."

At a separate time, it's easy to play a game that had you do it the right way. The smaller children are, the more they love these games. Maybe we would put three objects in the chair. I would then tell the child what to do. Of course I would say it in a fun way since we are playing a game. When Daddy says put the play horse down, you need to get the horse, say "Okay Daddy" and then put it down. If I say, ball, then say "Okay Daddy" and put it down. Play the game several times. Siblings often like to join in.

Remember that bad attitudes are associated with certain looks and murmuring words. We want to replace the dour face with a happy face and the upset noise with a bright 'Okay Daddy.'

Schedules & Routines

Once these routines are configured, they become a schedule. All we need to do is coordinate a time along with the routine. In this way the routine gets even more fixed, and habits are more deeply engrained because it happens the same time each day. This helps the parents as well as the children, especially when they are older and understand time. Punctuality is an important character quality that we want to develop in our children. Punctuality is keeping my word as to what time I will be there so that others are not inconvenienced but encouraged.

7:00	Rise and shine routine
7:30	Morning jobs (older children) & eat
8:00	Morning devotions
	and so forth

But remember that schedules and routines are to serve us. We need to occasionally remind our children that we can change schedules and routines because we made them. For example, if we regularly send the child to bed at a certain time, there might be a conflict with a special church meeting. We tell them that God is more important. So we change the schedule for that day. Perhaps we would give the youngest children a nap. Or maybe adjust the length of the nap. They stay up late, and we may adjust the morning schedule with a later rising time. There must be flexibility built into the schedule.

Although it seems that the child without routines is more flexible, the opposite is the truth. The child that has learned to comply with the parent's word can better adjust because he can trust the parent without a struggle. Furthermore, he has a regular schedule to get back into as soon as this segment is past.

Conclusion

We can train our child to do what we want. As parents we need to more clearly focus on God's goal for our children. After all He will keep us accountable for the way we train our child. We need to be faithful in what He has given us to do.

The best thing is that when we train our child well, it is fun to be with him or her at any time in any place. We are setting up a great foundation for being best friends when that little one grows up. Praise God for His special Word that instructs us to properly train our children!

#8 Study Questions

1. How do parents cultivate spoiled children?

2. List three things that the child learns when he is trained to refrain from grabbing.

3. What is the ideal time for training a young child?

4. Give one reason parents don't train their child to do what is proper (carry out good routines)?

5. How do you train a child to brush his teeth?

6. How do you train a child to fold his pajamas and put them away?

7. How about getting dressed?

8. What does your morning 'rise and shine' routine look like compared to the one above?

9. Explain a game you could play with the child to train him to come without fussing or running away.

10. Why is it important to train a child's attitudes as well as his actions?

Quiz: First-time Parents

What do first-time parents really know about babies?

1. Why do babies cry?

2. What are their physical needs?

3. What are their emotional needs?

4. What are the spiritual needs of the baby?

5. Do babies in the womb hear and respond?

6. What is the nature of the newborn like?

7. How much does the training of a child in the first three months influence the child's life?

8. Can a baby one month and older be trained?

9. Are babies a neutral or blank slate to be written on orally, spiritually, and intellectually?

10. What do babies need most?

11. Why does God give us babies?

12. What does God say about babies/young children?

13. Does a boy need circumcision? Why or why not?

14. How much does it cost to have a baby and raise it?

15. What are your hopes and dreams for your child?

16. What kind of child do you want?

17. Does saying "No" damage a child?

18. What's the best way to nourish them?

19. How do our understanding of marital roles affect our family life?

20. What is the world's attitude toward children?

Godly Beginnings for the Family QUIZ

Answers: First-time Parents

Brief Answers to the Quiz: What do first-time parents really know about babies?

1. **Why do babies cry?**

   Babies cry for numerous reasons including being wet, hungry, or tired; wanting attention, to be picked up, etc.

2. **What are the physical needs of infants?**

   A baby has numerous physical needs. A good starter list include warmth, food, secure place, sleep, and flexible routine.

3. **What are babies' emotional needs?**

   A baby's emotional needs include: love affection, peace, patient handling, and joy.

4. **What are the spiritual needs of your baby?**

   Your baby's spiritual needs include but are not limited to: orderliness, self-control, love, obedience, a fear of God, and honor toward parents. In one sense these physical, emotional and spiritual needs are very interrelated. We must not forget that.

5. *Do babies in the womb hear and respond?*

We see through John the Baptist in the womb that babies are attentive to the surroundings outside the womb. "And it came about that when Elizabeth heard Mary's greeting, the baby leaped in her womb; and Elizabeth was filled with the Holy Spirit" (Luke 1:41).

6. *What is the nature of the newborn like?*

The sinful nature of every child gives him or her a tendency to satisfy his or her own basic desires (i.e. flesh). As the child grows physically and emotionally, the child will become more and more adept at expressing this sinful nature.

7. *How much does the training of a child in the first three months influence the child's life?*

The training and love established by how the parents deal with and respond to the infant greatly influence what a child will later expect and shape how he or her will respond. These initial training has a life-time impact on the child.

8. *Can a baby one month and older be trained?*

Sure can. In fact, they will always be trained by how we handle them, for good or bad. We can think of this training through the general routines that we either establish or fail to establish.

9. *Are babies a neutral or blank slate to be written on orally, spiritually, or intellectually?*

Definitely not. They are embedded with different abilities, gifts and even depraved morally. We should not think of them as a blank tablet, which is going to be written upon. They have their personalities and a bent toward sin. As soon as they can express themselves, this selfish aspect becomes apparent. We must remember God has His own design and purpose for each child.

10. What do babies need most?

Babies need most parents who committed to constantly loving them even when they are irritable. This enables the children to have a positive and trusting attitude toward life in general. Through this love, a Christian parent can begin to communicate God's love and care to the child.

11. Why does God give us babies?

God gives parents babies to expose their sin and to help them grow. Through children, God expands his kingdom and reveal His glory as they become Christians and live out God's principles in their lives.

12. What does God say about babies and young children?

God clearly and repeatedly tells us that children are a blessing and a reward. Mankind is told to be fruitful. This means we should look at having many children as a good and godly action. God is intimately involved in the process of giving life. Each child is a miracle in that sense.

13. Does a boy need circumcision? Why or why not?

There is much to say on the topic of circumcision. It is complicated by hostility at times. Those that are anti-circumcision think it barbaric and unnatural. Others are confused with Biblical teaching and need. Biblically, it does not matter. It is probably better to be circumcised, but with present day hygiene, there seems to be very little real necessity.

14. How much does it cost to have a baby and raise him?

Although the world tells us that raising a child is well over a hundred thousand US dollars, we can raise a healthy God-fearing child with very little. God is content to provide the basics to each family. Formal education is a luxury and not a strict need.

15. *What are your hopes and dreams for your child?*

This differs for each parent. But it is very important to think through what one wants for the child. The more aware and honest you can get about your hopes, the more you and your spouse can understand why you think certain things are important for the child. These underlying differences can become potential hot spots for arguments if they go undetected.

16. *What kind of child do you want?*

Usually the parent thinks in terms of wealth, strength, and beauty. But the chief needs of a child are far different. A child really needs self-control, spirit of obedience, wisdom, ability to acknowledge his wrong and a devotion to God and commitment to help others.

17. *Does saying "No" damage a child?*

Definitely not. The opposite is true. If we refuse to say "No" to them then they will be damaged. By refusing certain things for them is the beginning of training. They will later in life need to personally say no to unhelpful things in order to please God and love mankind.

18. *What's the best way to nourish a baby?*

Breast-feeding is best way to nourish a baby. God has built this feeding process in for both nutrition, health, and emotional security. It is also easiest for the parents! Sometimes it is impossible for a mother to nurse the baby. The mother fortunately can find baby formula to help here, but it should not be considered a substitute if not necessary.

19. *How do our understanding of marital roles affect our family life?*

Because marital roles are not well-thought through, there are a lot of misunderstood expectations as to what the other spouse should do "to be loving." For example, who should get up at night with the baby the third time she cries? It is important for spouses to examine their expectations in light of God's Word. The world is sending out many erroneous messages. Only God's way is best.

20. What is the world's attitude toward children?

The world tends to hate or be indifferent to children. They pretend to love them, but they hate them by being willing to kill them through abortion[78], and ditch their upbringing to make more money. Children are often considered to be nuisances and inconveniences. These are all horrible responses. A baby is God's gift. A calling from our Creator. An important way of life. We as parents are charged to raise up this child for God's purpose. At the same time, we are totally blessed through each of our children as we train them and can enjoy their company and affection.

---

[78] "Researchers Uncover Hidden Risk Factor For Breast Cancer" www.care-net.org/ abundant-life-blog/researchers-uncover-a-hidden-cause-of-breast-cancer

Appendix 1:
Suggested Reading

There are many poorly executed books on parenting. Here are a few good ones!

Two of our other family-oriented books:

Building a Great Marriage: God's Design, Your Marriage![79] The harmony of one's marriage is one of the largest influences on a child's behavior.

Principles & Practices of Biblical Parenting: Raising Godly Children (This book focuses on training from two years and up.)[80]

BFF's Parenting Digital Library includes both our parenting books, audio/videos from a parenting seminar and more![81]

Other suggested books:

The War Against Population: The Economics and Ideology of World Population Control by Jacqueline R. Kasun Ignatius Press, 1999.

Gut and Psychology Syndrome: Natural Treatment for Autism, Dyspraxia, A.D.D., Dyslexia, A.D.H.D., Depression... (Nov 15, 2010) by Natasha Campbell-McBride. Medingorm Publishing, UK.

Unraveling the Mystery of Autism and Pervasive Developmental Disorder: A Mother's Story of Research & Recovery (Jan 8, 2002) by Karyn Seroussi and Ph.D. Bernard Rimland. Simon and Schuster.

Nourishing Traditions: The Cookbook that Challenges Politically Correct Nutrition and the Diet Dictocrats (2001) by Sally Fallon.

The Nourishing Traditions Book of Baby & Child Care (Mar 16, 2013) by Sally Fallon Morell and Thomas S. Cowan.

---

[79] http://www.foundationsforfreedom.net/Help/Store/Intros/BGMarriage.html

[80] http://www.foundationsforfreedom.net/Help/Store/Intros/Biblical_Parenting_Intro.html

[81] http://www.foundationsforfreedom.net/Help/Store/Intros/DLibrary-Parenting.html

Appendix 2: Infant Shots and Immunizations

Parents must not just accept what they are told regarding immunizations. There is a lot of contradictory data. Some of it we cannot well decipher due to big profit gains by the drug companies. There is concern with what is put in the vaccines, sometimes including heavy metals,[82] preservative in the vaccines given to infants, and even proteins from aborted babies.[83] Fortunately, Thimerosal is no longer used (but why they insisted it doesn't matter scares me),[84] but there remains a great concern of overwhelming the baby's immune system by giving them numerous vaccines so early on in life. I counted 24 recommended vaccines given to a child by 12 months old.[85]

Many parents, including ourselves, cannot totally trust our governments. Nor can we trust reports that claim vaccines are not connected to autism. They even want to vaccine our children to prevent the most infamous HPV sexual disease that is contracted through immorality (Gardasil vaccine). This would be bad enough except that there are many bad side affects.[86]

The danger of immunization ingredients is greatly increased when given to infants and small children before their systems have

[82] "If Your Doctor Insist..." www.preventdisease.com/news/12/050212_If-Your-Doctor-Insists-That-Vaccines-Are-Safe-Have-Them-Sign-This-Form.shtml

[83] "Warning: Many childhood vaccines contain aborted human fetal protein, DNA" www.naturalnews.com/038873_childhood_vaccines_aborted_babies_DNA.html

[84] "Thimerosal in Vaccines" www.cdc.gov/vaccinesafety/Concerns/thimerosal/index.html

[85] "2016 Recommended Vaccinations" www.cdc.gov/vaccines/parents/downloads/parent-ver-sch-0-6yrs.pdf

[86] "Gardasil: The Decision We Will Always Regret" healthimpactnews.com/2015/gardasil-the-decision-we-will-always-regret/

stabilized. It makes us pause to wonder whether harm is done to the body's immune system, especially the little babies! There is quite a debate over whether there is a real link between the MMR and autism. Since the government is convinced that the program must go on, then we cannot trust their presentations.

Summary

We are concerned with both the danger of the immunizations given to infants as well as whether or not they are really helpful in preventing disease. From our reading, we have less enthusiasm for the immunization programs than the government does. We realized something was very wrong when we were asked to sign a consent form for a child's immunization, in which the government in small print stated that they will not be liable for any complications due to the immunization. Isn't the FDA supposed to ensure that medications are safe? Something is very suspicious.

The problems do not seem so intense when older children have the immunizations. It is obvious that not all the data is in. We highly recommend all parents with little ones to at least postpone the immunizations and, if administered, spread them apart.

Appendix 3: About This Book

We (Paul & Linda) wrote this book from our personal experiences in birthing, raising, and providing early training for our eight children. We hope the advice found in this book will give each of you a good beginning!

In this book you will find biblical principles integrated with practical advice specifically geared toward expecting parents or those engaged in baby care. Each chapter has study questions appropriate for discussion either in a small group setting or as a couple.

Our 35+ years of marriage have been busy, yet filled with the joys of raising eight children. For us, family life has been enriching. The addition of grandchildren deepens the joy we have already found in our family, a joy that we want passed on to every family.

What should you look forward to discovering in *Godly Beginnings for the Family* besides chapter study questions and a quiz (and answers) titled, "What do first-time parents really know about babies?"

FAMILY

What is the family? What should our attitude be toward children? How do children fit into the lives of their parents?

EXPECTING

Before birth is the time for parents to get ready! What is childbirth like? What steps can parents take to get ready?

ARRIVAL

What should parents expect the first weeks after birth? Explanation and sharing helps parents properly handle the fast-changing family.

ROUTINES

Defines, describes, and discusses the important place for routines in a child's early training. Start right, end right!

About the Authors

Paul and Linda wrote this book from the personal experiences in birthing, raising, and providing early training for their eight children. With over 35 years of marriage, much pastoral experience, family counseling, and an international training of pastors, their commitment to the scriptures and ability to intertwine God's precious truths to daily life give hope and inspiration to many across the world.

Paul and his wife Linda continually see God's blessings unfold in their lives. With four grandchildren, their baby care experience has turned a different corner, and yet continues in the same ways by seeing God's blessings poured out into our family.

www.ingramcontent.com/pod-product-compliance
Lightning Source LLC
Chambersburg PA
CBHW071425090426
42737CB00011B/1568